THE

FORGIVENESS

EFFECT

About the Author

Francine Westgate is an inspirational speaker, teacher, and author. She holds her minister's license through One Way Churches International under the leadership of Bishop Lorenzo Hall and Bishop S.Y. Younger. She is the wife of Pastor William Westgate, Associate Pastor of the RAMP Church International. Together they have three sons and one granddaughter. Francine and her husband lead the married Couples ministry, where they teach couples how to maintain a healthy marriage by sharing their own personal experiences. Francine has a successful blog called "I Am M.O.R.E" and has two memoirs in the works, *In the Land of Canaan: A Little Girl's Giants* and *Fiddleheads*, where she shares how she overcame the crippling effects of childhood sexual abuse through hope and the power of forgiveness. Francine also shares her wisdom and knowledge as she leads the Refreshed Women's Group at the RAMP Church International in Lynchburg, VA. Francine continues to travel and teaches workshops on forgiveness, where she shares her story to empower the hurting and to help them view their wounds as a means to help others. Francine loves to study and teach the Word of God and is the director of the Christian Education Department for One Way Churches International.

Ways to contact the author:
Visit her website at www.francinewestgate.com.

THE
FORGIVENESS
EFFECT

Francine Westgate

*What if the question isn't **how** but **when?***

Editor's note

THE FORGIVENESS EFFECT. Copyright © 2022 by Francine Westgate. All rights reserved. Printed in the United States of America.

No part of this document may be reproduced or transmitted in any form or by any means, electronic, mechanical, photocopying, recording, or otherwise, without prior written permission of the author, Francine Westgate, and Fiddlehead Press, Lynchburg, VA.

Requests for permission to make copies of any part of the work should be submitted to www.francinewestgate.com.

Designed by Francine Westgate

Data

Name: Westgate, Francine, 1973—author.
Title: The Forgiveness Effect / Francine Westgate
Description: First edition.
Library of Congress Control Number: 2022918291
ISBN 979-8-9870340-1-9 (paperback)
ISBN 979-8-9870340-0-2 (eBook)
ISBN: 979-8-9870340-2-6 (Hardback)

Names and details may have been changed to protect the privacy of those mentioned in this publication. This publication is not intended as a substitute for the advice of health care professionals. The publication is based on the author's life experiences. Excerpts from her soon to be published memoirs may contain trauma triggers. Unless otherwise noted, all Scriptures are taken from the Holy Bible, King James Version (Public Domain)

10, 9, 8, 7, 6, 5, 4, 3, 2

PRAISE FOR THE FORGIVENESS EFFECT

"Francine Westgate is the new, global megaphone for freedom. This book is a real-time, fresh perspective on repurposing seasons of pain to live free. Francine's new approach to rethinking suffering is one of the most profound, biblical manuscripts I have ever read. Most propelling, Francine teaches us how to move to healthy and empowering spaces of forgiveness so that the glory of God can be activated and displayed in our daily lives. Thanks to Francine and her literary fortitude, I now fully embrace the difficulties of my past and see forgiveness as freedom. And this new spiritual liberation has initiated greater levels of global impact and influence in my career. Francine is the voice I have been waiting for and her debut book on forgiveness will do for you what it did for me...set you free!"

— Mary Millben,
Award-winning American Singer/Actress

"This is a moment in history. This book is anointed to set captives free. Francine Westgate in her genius paints a beautiful, griping, raw, deep, insightful, and inspiring picture as she connects her life, river drivers, and Jesus in a breathtaking guide to forgiveness."

— Jason Clark

"If 'forgiveness is for you not them' had a book that taught us this adage, "The Forgiveness Effect" would be it. Francine Westgate manages to teach about logging, forgiveness, love, and acceptance seamlessly while captivating and challenging the reader. Whether you feel like you need to forgive or not, if this has caught your eye it is worth taking the time to sit and stay a while. There is something here for everyone. I believe "The Forgiveness Effect" will transform your life and I am excited for what else is to come from the author."

— Karlissa Boyd

"This book is a deep soul-searching journey that will take you from the painful grips of trauma, and bring you to the foot of the Cross, with a revelation that forgiveness was the road you needed to get there."

— Aline Ehade, Licensed Professional Counselor

"Gripping, moving, and a powerful book of healing and wholeness. Francine Westgate takes the reader through a raw, yet beautiful journey of healing with the skills learned from the river driver attributes. I resonated with the weighted words on these pages and found direction in my healing process."

— Julyanna Collins

"The scriptural depth and context, the metaphorical references, and the similitude of this writing are mind-blowing. I truly experienced my own level of deliverance while reading this book, which I didn't even know I needed. Forgiveness is an underrated decision and often we breeze past it in life because it is easier to not deal with it. Well, this book paralyzed me for a moment, and I could not help but search my heart and open my mind and release forgiveness. This is a great and highly recommended read."

— Jasmine McKinney

"I believe it will be near impossible for you to put this book down once you begin reading, as it was for me. This book is not only revelatory, but it is an Education, a Revelation, and an Emancipation. It's an education in the intentionality of God and the true depth of His forgiveness of us. It is an irrefutable revelation of how little to do with those who hurt us, forgiveness was ever about. It is an emancipation as this book will provide you with the tools necessary to be set free from the poisonous, inadequate consolation, and empty promise of control that comes from unforgiveness."

—Will Wilson Jr.,
Associate Pastor of Elevation Church

This morning, as I put the finishing touches on the book, Ella Ruth asked me to share these words with you: "The love of God makes good Bible stories" - Words of wisdom from a 4-year-old.

This book is dedicated to my husband, Pastor William Westgate, and our three sons, Myles, Seth, and Ethan, and granddaughter, Ella Ruth. I love you, 3, 6, 9!

"It was labor intensive, but the river did most of the work"

—David Calder
A River Driver

ACKNOWLEDGMENTS

Many thanks…

David Calder. For sharing stories about the Last Log Drive on the Kennebec River in Maine and what it meant to be a river driver, and to your wife, Maureen, for taking my calls, and for being so kind to send pictures for me to use in the book.

Gary Noyce. A teacher, historian, and lover of all things river drivers. For taking the time to share his knowledge for this book.

Chuck Harris and Sandra Fayle for sharing your love of river driving and allowing me to use pictures from the West Branch Historical Boom House.

Christine Lockridge. Words cannot describe how near and dear you are to me. Thank you for the content editing, and for the daily check-ins and reminders to keep pushing. Keep writing. Keep revising.

Tracy Peade. For being the first one to read the completed rough draft, and for encouraging me along the way.

Pauline Gurske. For offering advice and insight and for reading every revised draft. For being a fierce big sister. A true river driver. Resilient in every way.

Charlene Farrington. For letting me ping ideas off you, and for believing in me, and well, for being my twin sister.

Mom and Dad. For allowing me to share my stories without having to candy coat them.

Charles Dodge. For simply being my baby brother.

Kelli Wilson. For allowing me to share your story of pain and suffering in the pages of this book. Lisa Harris. For allowing me to share our conversation, and for always being there for me.

Cassondra Richardson. For reading bits and pieces of the book, and for your love and support.

Erin Sutton. Karlissa Boyd. Joy Strout. For proofreading and editing. Tracye King. For help with the footnotes.

Krystal Crutchfield. For all of your feedback and encouragement.

Casey and Jason Clark. For your help and support. And for taking time out of your day to read and provide feedback.

Selena Roberts and LennaaMay Photography. For the photograph on the cover.

The Ramp Church International. For being my cheerleader and my rock, and for making me want to be a better version of myself. You are family. *I am because we are.*

And last, but not least, Emily Culver. For fixing the headers and footers. *I would still be trying to unlink them if it were not for you!*

THE

FORGIVENESS

EFFECT

RIVER DRIVER TOOLS

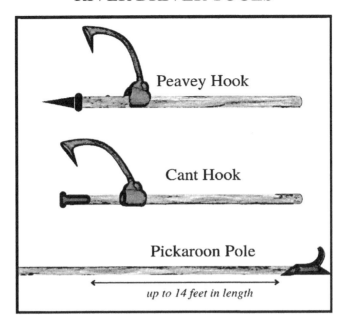

Peavey Hook

Cant Hook

Pickaroon Pole

up to 14 feet in length

FOREWORD

Every once in a while, someone comes along with a fresh take on an ancient struggle. Have you ever walked the bread aisle touching the loaves and come across one so fresh that it surprised you? Francine has combed over these words in such a way that they'll do just that, surprise you.

This is the type of book that, after you've finished it, you'll pay it a visit on the shelf for the memories.

There is this message of movement and hope that I'm anxious for readers to engage with. This is not so much a how to book as it is a where to book. Forgiveness is an ancient struggle, from Biblical perspectives to real life examples, Francine flips the light on and the bugs start to scatter.

Sometimes in life, someone works so hard for something and you watch their process and wonder, where did they get their resolve? That's a rhetorical question because I know the answer. God. He has placed *The Forgiveness Effect* in Francine's heart and she has beautifully shared her heart with us.

Years of ministry will teach you to be "quick to forgive." If the old adage "practice makes perfect is true," consider me a professional. However, while reading *The Forgiveness Effect*, I discovered that perhaps there was something I left back on the bank of the river, something that still needs some tending to. My prayer is that this book, or perhaps one might say manifesto, has an effect on you…a forgiveness effect.

Bishop S.Y. Younger

Pastor of the Ramp Church International, Presiding Prelate of One Way Churches International, Author of *Keep Going: 30 Day Devotional.*

River drivers with their pickaroon poles.

Photo credit and permission to use by David Calder, a
former river driver (in the white shirt looking at the camera

CONTENTS

INTRODUCTION

HOW TO REIMAGINE AND RECLAIM FORGIVENESS

To begin with, a bit about where this book comes from…

There's a native American proverb that says, *"The soul would have no rainbows if the eyes had no tears,"*[1] a one-liner that recapitulates my childhood well. At a young age, I made the correlation that sex and love were one and the same, and that affection came with strings like kites, and sneakers, and Yo-Yos's. I was six years old, the first time my uncle placed twenty-five cents in my hand, and said, "I love you. You're my good little girl," before pulling up his pants and tucking in his greasy mechanic shirt. His acts became more grievous when he began including my twin sister and disabled older sister, and even more so, when he started making a profit by selling us to his friends.

Around the age of ten, my uncle who lived next door moved away, and the person who moved in picked up where he left off. Then, when I was twelve, I was raped by a stranger in the woods. When he was done, he placed twenty-five dollars in my hand as if it was a peace-offering. *Mom said I had a sign on my forehead that let bad people know to pick me.* These things, and many others, left me hating myself and questioning God.

When I was thirteen, my aunt started attending a little church in Pittsfield, Maine, and, out of the blue, she invited me to go with her. At first, I said, *No,* but she insisted that *this* church wasn't like all the other churches, as if there was a different God over there then everywhere else, and I remember thinking,

Is God real?

If He is, then why didn't He help me? Why didn't He strike those men with His most powerful lightning bolt when I asked Him to? He must not love me.

My young mind was telling me, *stay home,* but my hurting heart was telling me, *go.*

So, I followed my heart and went.

The next morning, I woke up early and slipped on a mustard-colored skirt with two high slits (one up the front and one up the back—the only skirt I had), and waited at the window for my aunt to pick me up.

I'll never forget the Sunday school teacher's lesson on baptism in Jesus name. After class, I asked her if I could be baptized the way Peter preached and the way the people in the book of Acts were baptized. Her answer was a resounding, "Of course, Hun."

That evening I returned to the little church with my family, and I carried a long black duffle bag with bold white letters written across the side that said: MARLBORO. A bag that came in the mail after my mom redeemed the cigarette cartons she collected. Inside the Marlboro duffle bag was a tattered towel and a change of clothes. That night, when I came up out of the water, I felt like I'd been given a second chance, a new skin for my soul, and like the old song goes—new shoes for my brand new feet. Tears streamed down my cheeks in middle of the water creating rippling effects, and to this day, I've never been the same.

A few years later, at the age of sixteen, I was elected by the history department to represent Lawrence High School at Dirigo Girls State.

This was a week-long event where all the female delegates across the state of Maine gathered at the University of Maine in Orono to reenact town, county, and state government—we lobbied, made posters, rallied, and campaigned.

I can't recall which political party I was part of, whether it was *Courage* or *Honesty*, but I do recall wearing a bed sheet for a toga. One night, after a toga-wearing rally, I noticed a group of girls huddled to my right, so I made my way over to see what was going on. That's when I saw…

a
girl
on
the
front
row
in
a
low
chair,
as
though
she
was
sitting
Shiva.

Her brown hair covered her hands that covered her face that hid her grief. We all wore togas, but even through the toga I could see poverty and pain. The girl next to me told me *the* girl had been raped and was considering suicide.

It was as if I was looking in the mirror—*She was me!*

Feeling compelled, I pressed my way through the crowd to sit *Shiva* with her, and in solidarity whispered, "Me too! I was raped."

She lifted her head. Her tears watered her sandals.

"Really?" she sobbed.

"Really," I said.

Did I say that for me or for her? Was I being selfish? Can it be both, and I still be a Good Samaritan? I don't know. What I do know is, we weren't alone—somehow the suffering blurred the lines between heaven and earth and brought the Holy down. God sat *Shiva* with us.

It was there on the front row, beside a girl who's name I didn't know, that I decided to give my life to reclaiming the brokenhearted, the oppressed, and the marginalized by teaching them the power of forgiveness.

What is shiva? you ask.

Good question. *Shiva* means 'seven' in Hebrew. *Sitting Shiva* is the Jewish practice of expressing grief. It is a seven-day period, where the family sits together in low lying chairs to mourn the death of a close loved one.

But the girl on the front row didn't die? you say.

To that I add, then what is grief?

The short answer is,
Grief is a change that affects us.

The girl on the front row was grieving the person she was before she was raped.

"Grief is loss.

Loss is pain.

Pain is blame."[2]

Another answer is, "Grief is the root of all unforgiveness."[3]

But why am I writing this book? Well, I can't think of a better way to say it than how John Greene did, when he said, *"I write to show the fire in the darkness."*[4] I've been in Jonah's sandals and I know what it's like to be swallowed up by unforgiveness and spit out on the sandy shores of *How Did I Get Here?*

Maybe I'm the only one who's been in the belly of such a terrifying beast, but I seriously doubt it.

I know what you might be thinking. Isn't the market inundated with flyers and blogs and self-help books on *How to forgive yourself* and *How to forgive others?*

Maybe.

But none of them can give you the tools this book will give you. I know the ugly places bitterness and resentment can take you. I've been there!

If you're anything like me, the *how-to's* on forgiveness can be as frustrating as learning to tie your shoes and can seem as impossible as playing Pin the Tail on the Donkey while standing on your head in a gale storm.

As the age-old conundrum goes:

what do you do when you've prayed for and blessed your offender, but still feel stuck? What happens when you've tried every trick in the book, clicked your heels three times, and even thrown the book at them, but still wake up each morning in the same place of *How Did I get Here?*

I know what you're thinking,

How do you move past the hurt, before bitterness and resentment stick their hooks in you, before you are consumed by the injustice of it all, and before you find yourselves standing in a toxic pond,

neck-deep in sludge,

surrounded by mental marsh,

and leeches,

and lily pads,

and hungry alligators with sharp teeth,

while waiting for someone to pull you out of the razor-sharp jaws of offense? (Deep breath.)

The truth is, you're the only one who can do it, and this book is going to give you the tools you need. Starting with the wrong question you've been asking yourself and everyone else: How do I forgive? What if the question isn't how, but **when**?

Colleen Haggerty gave a Ted Talk titled, *Forgiving the Unforgivable.* She told the audience about how she lost her leg to a careless driver, and how years later, she called the driver to see if he would meet with her face to face. Colleen said, "I wanted him to see me. I wanted him to see me limp."[5]

Is that you?

Do you want the person who hurt you to *see* you limp?

I know for a long time, *that* was me.

My dog, Truitt, injured his foot on vacation a few years back, and for four days he hopped around on three legs. One night, as my husband and I were walking him, Truitt became preoccupied with sniffing, *as dog's do*, and suddenly he went from hopping on three legs to using all-fours.

I remember thinking,
Wait a minute?! You can walk?

That's when it hit me. Emotions have memory! Truitt couldn't move past the past until he allowed something else to take up his head space.

You've heard it said, *The past doesn't equal the future.* Well, that's true as long as you don't pitch your tent there!

But, we do this all the time, don't we? We stack up the offenses in our mind and allow them take up space. The problem with that is that it doesn't leave room to think about *much* else.

You know what I mean, right?
It's like what Dr. Phil said, *"Whoever said, 'Time heals all wounds,' lied. It's what you do with the time that heals the wounds."*[6]

In the letter to the Philippians, Paul tells us what things we should be stacking up. Things that are…
true,
honest,
just,
pure,
lovely,
and that are of a good report.
In other words, Paul is saying, think on positive things!

The truth is, we all have negative experiences. Whether it's the parent who abandoned us, the spouse who cheated on us, the family member who hurt us, the thief who robbed us, the liar who lied on us, the murderer, the child abuser, the rapist, the bigot, the judgmental saint, or the calloused leader. The Bible wants us to know that Paul wasn't exempt from it either.

2 Corinthians 11 lists some of those negatives Paul experienced on his journeys, starting with being whipped with thirty-nine lashes on five separate occasions by his own people, beaten on three separate occasions with rods, stoned once, shipwrecked, robbed, and falsely accused.

Wow! And I thought I had problems!

So then, why does Paul say,
But this one thing I do, forgetting those things which are behind, and reaching forth unto those things which are before.

Is Paul saying we should just leave all our memories behind and forget about all the negatives as though *they* never happened?

Yes and no. Memories make us human. *We can't find our shoes without it.*

Perhaps instead of stacking the negatives in our head, Paul is introducing a new concept—something edgy—something radical—something that has to do with forgiveness—a new way of looking at the hurts and pains and offenses and *turning* them over.

So, I ask, what if we treated the offenses like *logs* the way the river drivers do?

Did you say logs? And what's a river driver? you ask.

Well, before the invention of the logging truck, the river drivers were skilled lumberjacks whose job it was to deliver the logs to the mill by floating them downstream up to 100 miles away. Each log was, get this—valuable, and the more logs the river drivers delivered to the mill, the more the job was worth. The caveat being that the reward comes when you get the logs to the mill. Perhaps this is what Isaiah meant, *For your shame ye shall receive double.*

It's important to note that the river drivers were not just men, they were also women.

Really?
Yes.

The men were called River Jacks, and the women were called River Jills. During the 1940's, with many of the men away at war, the women took to the rivers, the factories, and even the baseball fields, like in the movie, *A League of their Own.*

There aren't any lumberjacks in the Bible, you say.

Wrong!

Gideon's name literally means *lumberjack!*

How cool is that?

The pages of the Bible are filled with skilled lumberjacks who, with watchfulness, worked and read the River of Life.

This book is designed to help you think and act like a river driver, to help you identify the *logs of unforgiveness* that are hindering the flow of the Spirit and creating log jams in your life. My desire is to give you the tools, the skills, and the understanding you need to push the *logs* downstream to the place of completion that God has for them.

The Spirit is always flowing but it's not the rivers job to get the logs to the Mill. You have to do the doing!

 So…

River Driver.

(Yes. That means you!)

Are you ready to move those *logs*?

Sound crazy?

Good.

Keep reading.

A river full of logs

Photo credit: West Branch Historical Preservation Committee,
http://themaineboomhouses.org/photos-from-the-past/

1

GOATS, DOGS & RIVER DRIVERS

"Many people have trouble with forgiveness because they have been taught it is a singular act to be completed in one sitting. That is not so. Forgiveness has many layers, many seasons"

— *Clarissa Pinkola Estes*

I WAS THREE, when the last log drive took place on the Kennebec River in Maine, back in 1976, just a few miles from where I grew up in Canaan. The log drive began when the last bit of ice melted on the Kennebec and lasted as late as December, when the river began to freeze over again.

The log drive started at Mooschead Lake, a hundred miles from my house, where the river drivers would prepare the logs in advance by cutting down trees, sawing off limbs, and stamping the ends of the logs with a letter or a symbol to indicate ownership. After that, they would shoot the logs onto the frozen lake with a log shooter or drag them onto the lake by a team of horses to wait for the ice to melt enough to use a tugboat. Finally, they would drag the 30,000 tons of logs held in booms across the lake to the mouth of the river. A boom was made by chaining 20-foot logs end-to-end. The boom would then be placed around the prepared logs, like a fence, keeping the floating logs together. All of this was done while there was still 4-feet of snow on the ground.[7]

Once the booms released the logs into the river, a crew of river drivers would work together to maneuver the logs downstream to Scott's Paper Mill in Winslow where, at times, the river would be 6-8 feet thick with logs and you couldn't see the river through the floating logs.[8]

The river drivers' job was to keep the 30,000 tons of logs flowing so as not to create a log jam, and to ensure safe arrival of the logs to the mill. The river drivers would build make-shift dams, known as splash dams, to flood fields, farms and pastures. Sometimes they would use dynamite to blast boulders, widen riverbanks, and clear log jams.[9]

The river drivers were agile and strong. They walked, balanced, and ran over the tops of floating logs. They skillfully steered flat-bottomed wooden boats through the raging rapids and around boulders and islands while standing up in the boat and directing the logs downstream with their pickaroon poles. When the logs got snagged by boulders, stranded in the shallows, or forced up on the riverbanks, the river drivers used the peavey hook to turn them over and free them.[10]

But wait! There's more.

After months of floating 30,000 tons of logs downstream, widening riverbanks, blasting boulders, clearing obstacles and debris, building splash dams, battling snow, ice and rain, and causing intentional but controlled flooding for the logs to pass down river, when the logs finally reached the mill, the river drivers would then trek back up the river to collect all the stray and stranded logs left behind. They would float the stray and stranded logs back downstream to the mill. This they called, *Cleaning the Rear*. Cleaning the rear was an important part of the process, because they only received payment for the logs that made it to the mill.[11]

That's interesting! But what do logs and river drivers have to do with forgiveness?

Well, I was thinking about the "Scapegoat" in the Old Testament recently: On the Day of Atonement, the high priest entered the tabernacle and sprinkled the blood of a spotless goat on the Mercy Seat in the Holy of Holies. Another goat, known as the scapegoat, was led away into the wilderness, symbolically carrying away the sins of the Israelites. Each year, for fifteen hundred years, the Jewish nation waited to see if the high priest would return from behind the veil. His return meant their sacrifice was accepted and that their sins were carried away or 'rolled ahead' for another year, that is, until the next annual Day of Atonement, when the process of forgiveness had to be renewed.

Suddenly, the image of their sins being pushed forward made me think of the *river drivers* pushing logs downstream with their pickaroon poles and peavey hooks, singing and shouting and carrying on. That's when it hit me!—there's a lesson to be had in how the river drivers worked the river and moved the logs downstream and how the Scapegoat moved sins forward for fifteen hundred years. The river drivers possessed certain tools and qualities and techniques that, if applied to our own lives in the area of forgiveness, would transform us from the inside out.

This book is about river drivers and scapegoats and log jams and two dogs and forgiveness.

Now that you know all that, let's talk about logs.

The logs are the offenses you are unwilling or unable to forgive or move past. They are the hard feelings, intense, painful, and negative emotions or traumatic experiences that take up headspace and cause you to hold grudges, lash out, and become consumed with revenge.

The word offense comes from the Greek word *skandalon*, meaning, a trap, a stumbling block, or a wrongdoing. The offense is the trigger that traps the unsuspecting victim.[12]

Offenses are unavoidable!

And because they are unavoidable, whether it is a single traumatic event or a collection of wrongs, the Scripture teaches us how to respond when offenses come, rather than how to feel. We may not be able to change how we feel right away, but we can control what we think about and what we *do* with those feelings when faced with offenses…just like the Canaanite woman in the Gospel of Matthew.

Right away, Matthew lets us know the Canaanite woman was from the wrong side of the tracks and she didn't have the right credentials to approach a group of Jewish men.

How do I know?

Because, back then, being Jewish meant you belonged to the in-crowd. This meant that you were God's chosen people and the apple of His eye. Being non-Jewish meant that you were NOT His chosen people and not the apple of His eye. A story that in various ways and to various people groups still exists today.

Maybe it's not a huge deal now, but, back then, women weren't allowed to approach men or ask them questions. There was an order: Jewish women were ranked below Jewish men, and non-Jewish men were ranked below Jewish women, and non-Jewish women were ranked below non-Jewish men.

So, in the Gospel of Matthew, this courageous woman from the wrong side of the tracks, who is the lowest on the totem pole, has a suffering daughter and cries out for help and this is the response she gets...

Log #1:
Jesus ignores her.

Log #2:
The disciples tell Jesus to get rid of her because she was pestering them.

Log #3:
Jesus tells her that He didn't come for her kind (a non-Jew).

Log #4:
Jesus calls her a dog.

But she doesn't let the little box checked *other* or the green card in her wallet stand in her way. She knows if she steers the logs down river to the place of completion she will be rewarded, and rather than skirt away with her tail between her legs, she falls to her knees and says, *True, Lord, but even the dogs eat the scraps that fall beneath their master's table.*

Matthew wants us to know that something more is going on just below the surface. Think *Charades.*

It's as if she is pointing to the Hebrew text and using Mephibosheth as her reference point to remind Jesus that, *yes*, dogs do eat crumbs from the master's table. *See!*

Mephibosheth, like the Canaanite woman, was from the wrong side of the tracks. He didn't start there. But, when his father Jonathan, and his grandfather king Saul were both killed, Mephibosheth ended up on the other side of the tracks in the barren wasteland of Lo-debar.

In that day, when a new king took over it was a common practice to exterminate the entire lineage of the previous king, including women and children. (A bit barbaric! I know! Picture *Game of Thrones*).

When Mephibosheth was just five years old his nurse, fearing for his life, took him and fled, and as she was fleeing, she dropped him, and he became lame in both feet. The Scripture doesn't say what type of fall he suffered or from what height he fell, but for him to become lame in both feet, it must have been from a very high place. (I picture the nurse tying bedsheets together and climbing out the castle window with Mephibosheth in her arms.)

Sometime later, the new king, David, who was once best friends with Jonathan, poses a question, *Is there anyone left of the lineage of Saul, that I may show him kindness for Jonathan's sake?*

After posing the question, David learned that his old friend Jonathan had a son named Mephibosheth who was hiding in Lo-debar with his nanny. So, David sent someone to fetch him and to bring him back to the castle. When Mephibosheth saw king David, he fell on his face in reverence, fearing he was about to be exterminated.

But David didn't exterminate him. Instead, he showed him kindness by restoring to Mephibosheth all the land that belonged to his father Jonathan, and to his grandfather Saul. If that wasn't enough, David gave Mephibosheth a seat at his table to eat bread with him continually, like a son.

Did you catch that? Mephibosheth was restored and given a seat at the master's table to eat bread forever.

Mephibosheth's response to the king's kindness was, *Who am I that you should look on such a dead dog such as myself?*

There are two things you should know...

First, the word Lo-debar means, *no pasture*. It was a barren place, a desert, or a place of exile. Not much bread to be had in Lo-debar, right?

Second, Mephibosheth's name has a duel meaning. It means, *out of the mouth of shame* and *out of the mouth of God*.[13]

Just one more thing before we circle back to the story of the Canaanite woman. Everything in the New Testament can be found in the Old Testament.

It's true.

Two thousand years ago when Jesus was healing the sick and feeding the multitudes, the New Testament didn't exist.

What do you mean, the New Testament didn't exist?

I mean, it didn't exist...yet!

What did they use for Scriptures then?

Well, I'm glad you asked.

The Jewish people used and still use what is called the Tanakh or the Hebrew Scriptures. (We know it as the Old Testament.)

It's important to know that when Jesus was speaking to His disciples, He was not quoting from the book of Acts or the Pauline epistles. He was simply pointing back to the Tanakh.

Jesus was a Jewish rabbi and the disciples were Jewish students, which means that they had large portions of the Tanakh committed to memory—entire books—thousands of verses—and they knew them like the back of their hand. Rather than count sheep to fall asleep, they quoted the Scriptures in the Old Testament that contained the word sheep.

In that day, and still today, Jewish rabbis used images, metaphors, and word pictures to push the students toward the text to uncover for themselves where the lesson for the day is coming from without the rabbi having to tell them.

So, it should come as no surprise when the Gospel of Matthew hints at and uses images and phrases to steer us back to the story of Mephibosheth with details like *dog* and *crumbs,* and such similarities as both being from the wrong side of the tracks, both being restored to a place of communion, and both dogs receiving bread from the master's table, so that the Jewish audience, i.e. the disciples might ask, "Where in the Hebrew Scriptures have we seen this scenario played out before?"

Okay, I see how Mephibosheth was restored, but how was the Canaanite woman restored? you ask.

That's easy…

The woman and her daughter were restored to community. Back in that day, if you had a blood disease, a skin disease, a birthmark, or were vexed by a devil, you were considered "unclean" and barred from the community. In Matthew's Gospel, the daughter of the woman was vexed by a devil, and because of it, the mother-daughter-duo lived in a shanty on the outskirts of town—possibly even a cave or in a graveyard.

At the end of the day, the woman's courage, strength, and perseverance paid off.

Jesus calls this river driver's pesky persistence great faith and Matthew makes sure to include the bit about her daughter being healed. The writer wants us to know her logs reached the Mill, the place of completion, the place where payment is made.

So, what do a bunch of river drivers in flannel shirts have to do with dogs and logs and forgiveness?

The answer is—
Everything!

The life of the river driver was centered around getting the logs to the mill.

Rain
or
shine
or
snow
or
ice.
The river drivers were strong and courageous, and just like the Canaanite woman, the Mill is the place of completion, the place where payment is made, the place where logs take new meaning, the place where pain and suffering transition from *the mouth of shame* to *the mouth of God.*

God wants to use your logs…all of them!

So, let me ask, do you have the strength, the courage, and the perseverance to steer your logs downstream long enough to get them to the Mill?

The Greatest River Driver to ever live uttered three words while suspended from two logs…*It is finished!* These words changed the past, the present, and the future for all humanity.

That means,

There is a place of completion for your logs. A place where the river drive ends, and the logs can be repurposed. It's the place where payment is made. A place where you receive double for your shame. But, you've got to get the bitterness, the hatred, and the resentment to Him first.

But you don't understand!

They haven't said they were sorry!

They hurt me in the worst imaginable way!

You don't know what they did to my loved one!

You're right! I don't know. What I do know is that forgiveness isn't predicated on how you feel, but how you respond. The Gospel writer omits how the Canaanite woman felt and shows us only what she did with her logs. It's because of her strength, courage, and perseverance that we are still talking about her two-thousand years later.

If God can do that for her with her logs, imagine what He can do for you with your logs. When you get them to the Mill. But to do that, you'll need the peavey hook and the pickaroon pole!

River drivers with peavey hooks and pickaroon poles

Photo credit and permission to use by David Calder, a former
river driver (in the white hat)

2

PICKAROON POLES & PEAVEY HOOKS

"If you wish to travel far and fast, travel light. Take off all your envies, jealousies, unforgiveness, selfishness, and fears

— Glenn Clark

PEOPLE ARE GOING to hurt you!—people you know—people you don't know—big people—little people—old people—young people—living people—dead people—good people—bad people— rich people—poor people—fake people—honest people—cynical people—polite people—grumpy people—loving people—rude people—quiet people—opinionated people—religious people— white people—brown people—black people—mixed people—all people!

Okay, you probably know that already!

But did you know that when *hurt* comes from the people you trust most in life, the people who are supposed to love you, the people who are supposed to keep you safe, it leaves you deeply, deeply wounded?

At an early age, I'd been seared by the hot iron of offense, and no matter how many times I put my thoughts through the spin cycle the yellow-singed-triangle remained. I've had many bouts with offense over the years, but this particular one left me reeling in emotional pain, and I did what most eleven-year-olds would do...I kicked grandma!

You can't be serious?!

Yes. Yes, I am. And, no, I'm not proud of it. The second thing I did was...

dog-eared,

stamped,

and filed it away,

just to remember,

never to forget!

For a long time, that offense cluttered the pages of my subconscious, cutting and weaving its way to the front of the line. It was like a reckless and impatient driver or a middle-aged woman in business attire who jumps ahead pretending not to notice the twenty-two people in front of her.

And yet, offense comes when you least expect, and it feels like *that* hair that wraps itself around your Parmesan chicken and screams, "Surprise!" leaving you tugging and pulling at it, like the red, and yellow, and green magician's scarf to get to the end and say, "Ta-dah"—only to find out that hair...doesn't belong to you!

And then, you do that thing we all do. You put out an APB on the wait staff, eyeballing them one-by-one, as a mental line-up to find the guilty party that matches the description—12" inches, straight, blonde.

This *dearly* offense came the day I decided to visit my grandmother next door. I hadn't been to her house in a while, at least not since my uncle, who was twenty at the time, pleaded guilty to sexually abusing me and got twenty-days in jail for it. When I entered the house, I saw my grandmother and my aunt leaning against the kitchen counter. They eyeballed me like I was that wait staff, and they'd found my hair.

Run!—Don't stay! I screamed in my little girl mind.

Ignoring the urge to flee, I tiptoed to my grandmother's rocking chair and sunk down in it. There I pretended not to notice the finger pointing and the loud whispers.

Suddenly, the whispers stopped, my aunt threw her hands on her hips, slid one flip-flop forward, and peered down her freckled nose at me. "Why don't you ask your grandmother if she wants you here?" she said, fast and angry.

I felt pummeled and disoriented. *It had never occurred to me that my grandmother might not want me around, since my uncle confessed and all.*

Choking back tears, I asked, "Is it alright, grandma?"

My grandmother's eyes darted around the kitchen as if chasing a bottle fly, and after a long awkward silence, she said, "For a few minutes, dear."

It was too late! Her silence told me everything I needed to know—

She didn't love me!

I wasn't wanted!

I didn't belong!

So, without thinking, I sprang from the rocking chair, made a beeline across the yellow brick linoleum, drew back my foot and kicked her in the shin with my hard-nosed Saddle shoe.

And since then, I've spent a lot of moments pulling the petals off the daisy in my head and doing the *she loves me—she loves me not— she loves me—she loves me not* thing, all the while *remembering not to forget* the shame and the humiliation and the rejection of that day.

Remembering…
I'm not good enough!

Remembering…
I'm not wanted!

Remembering…
I hurt grandma!

HOW YOU REMEMBER MATTERS

Have you ever tied a string around your finger just to remember not to forget something? If so, have you ever wondered where the idea came from?

I have.

According to the book of Numbers, the Jewish people are a people called to *remember.* God instructed Moses to have the people hang tassels from the four corners of their garments, so that when they look on the blue string in the tassels, they will remember the commandments of the LORD, and do them, so they can be holy.

The tassels, which are called *tzitzit,* hang from the corners of the *tallit,* otherwise known as the Jewish prayer shawl. Each tassel is made by threading four strings through a hole and looping them over to total eight strings. Each tassel includes one blue string, three white strings, and five double knots. The double knots represent the first five books of the Bible, otherwise known as Torah (Genesis, Exodus, Leviticus, Numbers, and Deuteronomy). Each tassel is bound together by the longer blue string with a specific number of intricate wraps.

In Hebrew all numbers have meaning, and all letters have numeric value. According to Jewish resources, "The eight strings and five knots are a physical representation of the Torah's 613 mitzvahs. It works like this: Each letter in the Hebrew alphabet has a corresponding numerical value (*gematria*). The numerical values of the five letters that comprise the Hebrew word *tzitzit* add up to 600. Add the eight strings and five knots of each tassel, and the total is 613."[14]

The blue string is there to remind the Jewish people of the Divine. I love that part—

Tekhelet is the word for the blue dye they used. This expensive dye came from a sea creature that lived in the Mediterranean Sea, called *chilazon.* The blue string is two inches longer than all the other strings in the tassel and is called the *shamash.* The purpose of the *shamash* is to join the white strings into a single stronger cord. The word *Shamash* in Hebrew means, "attendant or caretaker."[15]

Pretty cool, eh?

Blue string…Attendant…Caretaker…

I can't help but think of Jesus' high priestly prayer in John 17, *That they may be one as we are one.*

Now, back to the whole tie-a-string-around-your-finger thing.

Way back then, and still today, during a Jewish prayer service, the Jewish people wind the tassels around their fingers in an intricate manner as they pray and reflect on the commandments of the LORD contained in the Torah.

From this you can see how the Jewish people are a people called to remember and how that the blue string invites them to do just that. After all, the very One inviting them to remember, *also* remembers.

Now let's look at the word 'remember.' The first time it is used in the Hebrew Scripture is in Genesis, otherwise known as the book of Beginnings, when *God remembered Noah* in Genesis 8. In the Hebrew, the name Noah means, *rest, peace, comfort.* Thousands of years after the flood, the Apostle Peter writes,

Noah was the eighth person saved by water.

Why is this important?

As mentioned, in the Hebrew language all numbers have symbols and meanings attached to them. The number *eight* signifies new beginnings.

The *eighth* miracle recorded in the Gospel of John is the resurrection of Jesus, i.e. new beginnings. In John 14, we find Jesus preparing His disciples for His impending death, saying,

I go to prepare a place for you. And if I go and prepare a place for you, I will come again, and receive you unto myself; that where I am, there ye may be also.

In verse 18, He gives this clarifying line,
I will not leave you comfortless; I will come to you.

The word *comfortless* comes from the Greek word *orphanos*, which means, "orphan, fatherless, abandoned."[17]

Essentially, what Jesus is telling them is "Don't worry, boys! I won't leave you *fatherless*. I will come to you."

Jesus' relationship with His disciples is a matter of *presence*. The invisible God was physically present with His people through the body of His Son just as He was physically present with His people through the tabernacle in the wilderness.

Then, just eight verses later, we see Jesus telling His disciples that the Comforter, which is the Holy Ghost, will come in His name.

Do you see how huge this is?

Jesus is showing the disciples that right now He dwells with them, but He must go away so that He can return in a new form and live in them.

The Apostle Paul is a Jewish Christian with a monotheistic foundation and writes this to the church at Ephesus: *There is one Spirit.* A reiteration of what he already told the church at Corinth,

"Now the Lord is that Spirit: and where the Spirit of the Lord is, there is liberty."

Since there is only one Spirit and God is a spirit, here are some of the ways the Scripture describes the *one* Spirit of God:

Holy Ghost.
Fire.
Dove.
Spirit of Truth.
Peace.
Counsellor.
Helper.
Intercessor.
Strengthener.
Power.
Dynamite.
Gift.
Cloven tongues.
Tongues of angels.
Comforter.
Rivers of living water.
Advocate.
Oil.
New wine.
The list goes on.

These descriptions remind me of the *blue* string. We'll get back to it in a minute. But first, let's look at some of the language the Bible uses to describe the one Spirit now living and working in us:

Spirit of Christ,
Holy Spirit,
Holy Ghost,
Spirit of truth,

Spirit of adoption,
Holy Spirit of promise,
Eternal Spirit,
and
God.

Since we have *just* one Spirit working in us and through us, and what's above are some descriptions of *that* Spirit, we shouldn't be surprised when Jesus gives His disciples the heads up that when He departs, He will come back as the Comforter. When He does, He will teach them all things and bring all things to their *remembrance,* whatsoever He had already said unto them.

There's *that* word again—*remember*, which takes me back to when it was first mentioned in Genesis 8, when *God remembered Noah*, the eighth person saved by water.

This is a big deal! Jesus is connecting the dots for them.
Eight strings.
Eighth miracle.
Eighth person.

Remembering was and is a vital part of Jewish living, so much so, that Jesus blesses and serves bread and wine on Passover just before His death, otherwise known as the Last Supper. And makes the conversation about Himself, telling the disciples, *This do in remembrance of me.* This is a new idea. Jesus takes what always was and makes it about Himself. Suddenly, the Egyptian Passover which the Jewish people observed collectively for fifteen hundred years was no longer about *that* lamb and *that* Exodus but was about *this* Lamb and *this* Exodus that was about to happen. Reiterating that He is *the God who remembers.*

Jesus is opening their eyes to the Divine by inviting them to remember the *One* blessing and breaking bread with them. Through

21

their remembrance, their minds will be kept in perfect peace, because they trust Him.

Because when they remember Him, they remember Torah...
The Word became flesh.

Because when they remember Him, they remember the Father...
I and my Father are one.

Because when they remember Him, they remember the Holy Ghost...
I will not leave you comfortless: I will come to you.

How is this possible?

Because these three are One...Because in Jesus dwells all the fullness of the godhead bodily...Because Ephesians tells us there is...
one body,
one Spirit,
one hope of your calling,
one Lord,
one faith,
one baptism,
one God and Father of all, who is above all, and through all, and in you all.

(God's words, not mine.)

And because there is one blue string that reconciles all things to God.

The string is a reminder. The table is a reminder. The bread is a reminder. The cup is a reminder.

And that's not all...

Our remembering has everything to do with forgiveness because forgiveness is Divine. It's God's idea. If there is no forgiveness, there is no peace. Through the work on the cross, Jesus broke down the middle wall of partition between us, and through Him we have the forgiveness of sins.

So then, it would make sense to say, when it comes to the sacred space between our ears what we think about and *how* we remember matters.

Take this verse from Philippians 2,
Let this mind be in you, which was also in Christ Jesus.

Or this line from Romans 12,
Do not conform to the pattern of this world, but be transformed by the renewing of your mind...[18]

This is river driver language.

A skilled river driver knows how to read the river and what obstacles and debris to look for in order to prevent logs jams. The meaning we give to any significant memory can be stored in one of two ways. Either as a treasure or as a trauma.

How we categorize a memory, matters. For example, I no longer have 'childhood sexual abuse' dog-eared, stamped, and filed away under *Trauma*. Am I saying that if I had it to do all over again that I would choose sexual abuse for myself? No. Not at all. But it happened and I can't change that. And now, because of it, I get to share my story and help others. This is what I mean by getting the logs to the Mill. The Mill is where the logs get repurposed. A single traumatic event or the collection of wrongs can become a treasure when you realize your suffering has a purpose. Purpose comes alive when the traumatic memory is converted. Recategorized. Repurposed. Recapitulated. Renewed.

HOW NOT TO REMEMBER

The Hebrew Scripture records the Jewish people complaining about the things they weren't getting in the wilderness and rehearsing what they missed about Egypt. Saying things like,

We remember the fish that we ate freely in Egypt,
the cucumbers,
the melons,
the leeks,
the onions,
and the garlic;
but now our whole being is dried up; there is nothing at all except this manna before our eyes![19]

Since memory makes us human and we can't find our shoes without it, the problem wasn't **what** they were remembering, it was **how** they were remembering and the meaning they were giving it. They were not collectively remembering how God brought them out of bondage with the spoils of Egypt on their backs or how God parted the Red Sea and they walked across on dry ground or how God destroyed Pharaoh's army when the waters closed in on them or how their shoes never wore out or how God provided daily bread for them. Instead, they were remembering all the things they didn't have since leaving Egypt and ruminating in the negative.

There is a verse in the book of Acts that tells us that in their hearts, Israel turned back to Egypt. Brené Brown says in her book, *Daring Greatly* that "Nostalgia is also a dangerous form of comparison."[20] The Jewish people edited and revised their story so much that they believed they had it better in Egypt, in the place of affliction, in the shackles of bondage under the thumb of Pharaoh.

In other words, *how* they remembered caused them to stack up the negatives in their mind and in their heart, and although they were not physically back there in Egypt, their *remembering* put them there.

We do this all the time, don't we?

The past becomes present through our remembering. *Memory has emotion.* And emotion evokes from us one of two responses, treasure or trauma. The harm with nostalgia is that we can edit ourselves right out of rest, joy, and peace and right back into bondage.

And because memory has emotion, Paul reminds the church in Colossians to guard their thoughts by setting their affection on things above and not on things below.

Why does Paul do this?

Well, because thoughts are things.

In fact, Paul writes,

That the Lord Jesus the same night in which he was betrayed took bread: and when he had given thanks, he brake it and said, Take, eat: this is my body, which is broken for you: this do in remembrance of me. After the same manner also he took the cup, when he had supped, saying, this cup is the new testament in my blood: this do ye, as oft as ye drink it, in remembrance of me. For as often as ye eat this bread, and drink this cup, ye do shew the Lord's death till he come.

Paul invites the church to remember.

And why does he do this? What does all of this have to do with forgiveness?

Good question.

The answer is—
Everything!

And here's why...

Because as humans we have the tendency to store up the things that hurt us. Not only do we store them up, but we want those who hurt us to remember the pain they caused, i.e. *that* eye roll—cold shoulder—whispers—Facebook post.

Thoughts have the power to shape the landscape of our mind in a positive or a negative way—we are the landscapers and ultimately, we determine what our mental landscape looks like. At some point, we have to take accountability and stop blaming others for where we're at.

Which takes us to Proverbs,

For as he [a man] thinketh in his heart, so is he—literally!

Contrast that with the past becoming present in how we remember. Due to emotions having memory, it's easy to stack up the negatives in our mind, and in our body, whether it be a single offense or a collection of offenses, thus, restricting the flow of the Spirit, which then cuts off rest, joy, and peace. This causing us to become a former shell of ourselves. When that happens, all we have left is torment, anguish and bondage, which masquerades as bitterness, anger, and judgment; hurting those we love in the crossfire.

Not to mention that what we dog-ear, stamp, and file away has the ability to change the shape of our DNA.

A study done by The Institute of HeartMath showed how toxic thinking and negative emotions impact the DNA Code by causing it to tighten up and shrink.[21] According to Dr. Caroline Leaf, "Our brain is changing moment by moment as we are thinking. By our thinking and choosing, we are redesigning the landscape of our brain.[22]

In other words, when we dwell on the negative and traumatic event, the wrongdoing, the false accusation, the injustice—it restricts, tightens, and limits the anointing and the fruit of the Spirit in our life. It limits love. It limits joy. And it limits peace, to name a few. The need for justice is an all-consuming one. If we are not careful, it will take up our mental space with negative thoughts and feelings. That is why we must forgive. Another reason why the Apostle Paul writes to the church in Thessalonica this,

Quench not the Spirit.

Or to put it another way,
Do not extinguish the Spirit.[23]

Or to put it another way,
Don't put out the Spirit's fire.

Then Paul adds,
Hold fast to that which is good.

Recently, I was watching an old clip of a log drive, and one of the river drivers working the river, said, "A log drive wasn't all about well-behaved logs that flowed downriver without much work. All too frequently the rushing and bucking logs pitched and nudged each other, rubbing and bumping and creating diversions with what seemed like an almost human obstinacy to go their own individual way."

Sounds like us, doesn't it? When it comes to human nature, we can be as stubborn as a river full of bucking and nudging logs, and rather than follow peace, we go our own individual way.

Awareness plays a part in renewing the mind. Much of our mental anguish and torment can be directly linked to the unwillingness to forgive. If David were a river driver, his words in Psalm 51, *Create in me a clean heart, O God; and renew a right spirit within me*, might sound more like this, "Clear all obstacles and debris that cause log jams, so your Spirit can flow without restriction in me."

A large portion of the New Testament language is geared toward forgiveness, like "take up your cross daily," "bless them which persecute you," "pray for them which despitefully use you," "love your enemies," "daily bread," "do not let the sun go down on your anger," "be kind," "be tenderhearted," "be ministers of reconciliation," "leave your gift there before the altar," "I will give you rest," "endeavoring to keep the unity of the Spirit in the bond of peace," "be ye therefore perfect, even as your Father which is in heaven is perfect," "follow peace with all men," "bless, and curse not," and yes, even this, "judge not, that ye be not judged." Which we'll get to later in the book.

Since emotions are connected to memory, we may not always remember what someone said, but we'll always remember how they made us feel. And out of the need for self-preservation, we can hold onto to grudges long past their expiration date, sitting in our feelings until bitterness swallows us up, and all we have left is stale bread and darkness.

And if we are not careful, we can allow the negative experiences and feelings to dictate which *logs* to hold onto, and which *logs* to steer. *I'll forgive her for what she said. I won't forgive him for what he did.* **But remember...God wants all our logs!** As a river driver, we must work hard and fast to keep the rushing and bucking logs of offense moving downstream, so as not to create a log jam.

It takes skill.

It takes strength.

It takes awareness.

It takes resilience.

It takes empathy.

It takes perseverance.

Tony Robbins said something that has stuck with me since I heard it.

He said, "The meaning of communication is the response you get, and that all responses can be categorized in one of two ways: a loving response or a cry for help, and that cry for help is oftentimes met with a cry for help."[24]

Here, let me show you what he means...

After my uncle went to jail, the court mandated that my family and I attend family counseling. One of the exercises the therapist gave us to do as a family was to practice using kind words with each other. *Something we didn't do well.* So, after the first session, my mom surprised me at the kitchen sink with the words, 'I love you.' I knew she did, but I wasn't accustomed to hearing her say it. The surprise quickly turned into vulnerability which turned into anger which resulted in me saying, "Yeah, sure you do!" **My response**

was an emotional barrier that stemmed from a painful memory that manifested as a defense mechanism.

Profound…huh?

Looking back, I can see Tony Robbins was right. I wanted desperately to tell my mom, *I love you* back, but that was not what I communicated. What I didn't realize, at least not until I heard him say it was that my response was a cry for help. Mom's words made me feel vulnerable and afraid. What Mom didn't know was that my uncle who hurt me would tell me how much he loved me. So, when she told me she loved me, it triggered the trauma and caused me to remember the pain, making the two events one. *This was really about that—cause and effect.*

LOG BOOMS

Now let's talk about log booms. During the winter months, the river drivers would cut down trees and prepare the logs in advance for the spring thaw. First, by stripping them of their limbs, second, by stamping the end of each log with an emblem to indicate ownership, and third, by shooting them onto the frozen lake with a log shooter to wait for the ice to melt enough for a tugboat to be able to pull the log boom across the lake.

What is a log boom? you ask.

A log boom was the river driver's method of corralling the logs (also known as a fence or a bag). The river drivers linked together 20-foot logs end-to-end with chains, then placed the booms around the logs to keep them together.

The booms were not just used on lakes at the start of the logging season, but they were used at different junctures of the drive to corral the logs. The river drivers worked 15-hour days, sometimes more, and they would corral the logs in booms at the logging camp overnight, while they slept.

We do this all the time, don't we?

We corral the logs in mental booms as we sleep. In the evening, when we go to bed, and in the morning, when we wake up, the *logs* are there to remind us of the offenses, the pain, the suffering, and the injustices.

Mental Booms hold the logs: the negative experiences, hard feelings, heightened emotions, and traumas stored in our bodies and in or our nervous systems, which is why we may not remember what someone said, but we will always remember the negative or the positive extreme of how they made us feel.

There are at least three types of mental booms: Shock, Generational, and Bias.

Shock Booms are the negative emotions caused by traumatic experiences: a car accident, a phone call, sudden loss, natural disasters, abuse of any kind, and other acts of violence resulting in intense pain or a collection of offenses.

Generational Booms are the adverse effects, negative emotions and experiences, major injustices or trauma passed down through generations with which there is an increased probability of mental health disorders associated with genetics.

Bias Booms are the negative emotions, experiences, or trauma associated with a specific people group, culture, religion, tradition, geographical location, and language, whether real or perceived, resulting in prejudice, social injustice, person-to-person injustice, discrimination, and lack of integration.

IN AN INTERVIEW with Mark Biltz, Rabbi Pesach Wolicki said that "Jews have a very strong emotional memory. It's good, but it can also get in the way. Building bridges with Christians can be difficult. The Jews say things like, 'Look what they did to us during the Spanish Inquisition or the crusades' and the Christians say things like, 'You know you killed my Jesus.' Emotional barriers that stem from a historical memory."[25]

Joel Osteen writes in his book *Become a Better You*,

"I read of an interesting study done in 1993 by the United States military. They were curious about what traits get passed down from one generation to the next. We know that our physical traits do. What about emotional, mental, and spiritual characteristics? What about bad attitudes and addictions? Or what about good qualities such as integrity, compassion, and godliness? Can they be passed down as well.

The researchers extracted some white blood cells from a volunteer and they carefully placed them in a test tube. They then put a probe from a lie detector machine down in that test tube, to measure the person's emotional response.

Next, they instructed this same volunteer to go a couple of doors down and watch some violent scenes from an old war movie on television. When this man watched the scenes, even though the blood that was being tested was in another room, when he got all uptight and tense, that lie detector test shot off the page. It was detecting his emotional response even though the blood was no longer in his body. The experimenters did this with person after person with the same results. They concluded that the blood cells seem to "remember" where they came from."[26]

There is an interesting article written by Helen Thomson in *The Guardian* of a study done at Mount Sinai hospital in New York. The study included Jewish men and women who were Holocaust survivors. It found that trauma suffered by the men and women created a genetic change that could be passed down. The study concluded that one person's life experience can affect future generations. The study also looked at the genes of the survivor's children and determined that they had an increased probability of mental illness, namely, stress disorders. The head researcher said, "The gene changes in the children could only be attributed to Holocaust exposure in the parents."[27]

In the same article, Helen Thomson included a study done on male mice. A team of researchers at Emory University in Atlanta taught mice to fear the scent of cherry blossoms by giving them a small amount of electric shock each time they sniffed at a blossom. It didn't take long for the mice to link pain and scent. Thomson writes, "Despite never having encountered the smell of cherry blossom, the offspring of these mice had the same fearful response to the smell – shuddering when they came in contact with it."[28]

In all the Apostle Paul's letters to the churches, he never promised we would escape pain and suffering. He simply said, God would use it for good. Like when I said, "Me, too!" at Dirigo Girl's State to a young rape victim, or universally speaking, when Christ suffered and died.

It is possible to become ensnared by bitterness and resentment and forget that the Savior of the world came to break patterns and release the logs in the booms, so that the Spirit can flow to us and through us and so we can be free of bondage. *The Kingdom of heaven is at hand.* This means, abundant life is available here and now. All it takes is a decision. The river drivers didn't allow their feelings to dictate when to move the logs. Being a river driver is rewarding, but it's not easy. It takes practice, awareness, faith, and the right tools to push and steer the *logs of offense* downstream to the Mill.

THE TOOLS OF A RIVER DRIVER

The river drivers were agile, strong, and extremely fast footed. They had perfect balance which made it possible for them to run and walk over the tops of floating logs and maneuver flat-bottomed wooden boats through rapids and around boulders while standing up, pushing and steering logs downstream with their *pickaroon poles.* When logs got snagged by boulders or stranded on the riverbanks, the river drivers used their *peavey hooks* to turn the logs over and free them.

As a river driver, it's essential to know everything natural has a spiritual parallel. What I mean by that is, just as you hunger physically, you hunger spiritually; you thirst physically, you thirst spiritually; there are stop signs in the natural, there are stop signs in the spiritual.

In the natural, river drivers used peavey hooks and pickaroon poles to move the logs downstream. Let's look at the natural and spiritual parallels of these tools.

A. *In the Natural:*

The **Peavey hook** is a long sturdy pole with a thick point and a hook on the end.[29] The river drivers used it to roll the logs that were stuck or stranded. The tool has a thick spear-like tip for separating logs. The tip sticks in the ground and provides better leverage for maneuvering and separating logs. The hook on the end is called the 'dog leg' and is used to grab stranded and stray logs and turn them over. The 'dog leg' was used to break up log jams.

B. *In the Spiritual:*

The **peavey hook** is the ability to turn the offense over and look at it through the lens of empathy, compassion, and understanding. Said another way—it is *Fighting with Empathy, Fighting Fair,* or what Jesus would call, going the extra mile. It's the ability to put the other persons sandals on and see it from their perspective. It is the

34

awareness piece that makes it possible to respond to a 'cry for help' with a loving response. By turning the offense over and looking at it differently, we replace negative emotions and thoughts with positive emotions and thoughts, lessening the emotional pain and making it easier to forgive the injustice.

A. In the Natural:

The original **Pickaroon Pole**, also known as the Pike-Pole or the Pick-Pole used by a river driver was a long pole 10,12,14 foot in length with a thick iron spike on the tip that the river drivers used to push and steer the logs downstream.[30] It was used to keep the logs out in front of the flat-bottomed wooden boats and moving forward. The pole itself is made from Ash wood. Ash is a flexible wood that bends under pressure, so it doesn't break. The longer lengths were used to push the logs through make-shift dams, called splash dams, or separate the logs into booms at the mill based on the company logo or markings found on the end of each log that was made by an axe prior to the log drive season.

B. In the Spiritual:

The **pickaroon pole** is flexible and bends under pressure to prevent breakage. The long pole helps maneuver logs through difficult places. It is the tool used to push the *logs of offense* downstream to prevent log jams and to keep the logs moving in a forward motion toward the Mill, to the place of completion, where God can repurpose them for His glory.

PAUL WRITES TO the church in Rome and says this, *For when we were yet without strength, in due time Christ died for the ungodly,* and to the church in Ephesus, he writes, *Be kind to one another, tenderhearted, forgiving one another, even as God in Christ forgave you.*

Incredible, huh? While we were weak and powerless Christ forgave us, and because He forgave us, we ought to forgive one another.

Forgiveness is the crowning achievement of love. It's one of the two great equalizers. Suffering being the other. Forgiveness is Divine. It transcends thought and reason and clings to the rough edges and ugly places. On the cross, Jesus said, *Father, forgive them; for they know not what they do.* The Savior of the World didn't allow the pain of the cross to dictate whether He should forgive the soldiers or not. Therefore, setting the example for us, that forgiveness isn't predicated on an apology or an acknowledgement of some sort, but on the love of God in Christ.

Stop asking yourself and others, "How to forgive?" It's not how, it's **when**—when you get the logs to the Mill, then God will use them.

Two river drivers watching a crew of river drivers clear a wing jam before it becomes a log jam

Photo credit: West Branch Historical Preservation Committee,
http://themaineboomhouses.org/photos-from-the-past/

3

SPLASH DAMS & THREE JAMS

"Everyone says forgiveness is a lovely idea, until they have something to forgive"

– C.S. Lewis

THE RIVER DRIVERS' main job was to keep the 30,000 tons of logs floating downstream so as not to create a log jam. The river drivers did whatever was necessary to ensure the logs safe arrival to the mill. The whatever included building splash dams and sluice gates. A splash dam was a temporary dam constructed out of wood to raise the water level in smaller streams for the logs to safely maneuver downstream. When necessary, the river drivers also used dynamite to blast boulders, widen riverbanks, and clear log jams.

A single log jam could stop the flow of the river and back up the logs for miles, causing extensive damage to surrounding farmlands, crops, and cattle, leading to lawsuits against the logging company.

It's what the river drivers didn't want to happen!

The river drivers worked in crews and took on many roles. One crew followed the logs downstream in flat-bottomed wooden boats, pushing and steering the logs with their pickaroon poles. While, another crew, called the *Elite Jam*, worked ahead of the logs to keep the logs moving. A third crew came behind the first crew to *clean the rear* (a process we will get to later). But for now, let's talk about the Elite Jam. Their job was to identify potential risks and prevent log jams from happening by clearing all obstacles and debris so that the logs wouldn't get snagged on boulders, branches, and islands in middle of the river as they passed downriver. There were three types of jams that the *Elite Jam* watched for:

Wing Jams,
Center Jams,
and Log Jams.[31]

AS YOU KNOW, everything natural has a spiritual parallel, and as a river driver, you are responsible for getting your logs to the Mill—there is no lead crew, cleanup crew, or pushing and steering crew outside of YOU! These are your logs, and this is your process. With that being said, let's talk about the three jams you should be watching for.

A. In the Natural

The **Wing Jam** is when logs get snagged by trees and boulders on the embankment or on the shoulder of the river and cause other logs to get backed up in the river to form a point. At the first sight of a wing jam beginning to form, the river drivers worked hard and fast to break up the logs before they stretched across the river to the other side and stopped the flow of the river. Because if the river stopped flowing, the logs stopped flowing. In the event of a wing jam, the River Driver would use the pickaroon pole to separate the logs and break up the potential log jam.

B. In the Spiritual

The **Wing Jam** is the *Right Jam*. It focuses on the injustices, whether true or perceived. It's when you feel you didn't do anything wrong and you maintain the *right* to be bitter, to hold a grudge, or to seek revenge. It's the "It's not fair!" "I want restitution!" "I want everyone to know what they did to me," "I'm right and they're wrong" tape that plays over and over in your head. The injustice can either be against an individual or a collective group, system, or institution. A wing jam can quickly turn into a log jam and leave you feeling like an empty shell even when you are right.

A. In the Natural

The **Center Jam** is when logs get hung up on trees and boulders in the middle of the river. A center jam can sometimes take a team of river drivers a day's work to clear. The logs had to be picked off one by one, thousands of tons of them. The river drivers would use the thick metal point on the end of the pickaroon pole to separate the logs and use the peavey hook to turn logs over to get them unstuck.

B. In the Spiritual

The **Center Jam** is the "What about me?" jam. It forms when you can't get *you* off your mind long enough to get out of your own way. It's the everything is *happening to me* attitude that causes you to get hung up and stay hung up. It's the mindset that negative attention is better than no attention. The center jam is the insatiable desire to be seen and heard.

A. In the Natural:

The **Log Jam** can occur quickly from a wing jam or a center jam. The river driver must work hard and fast to clear the wing jam or the center jam in order to prevent a full-on log jam. A log jam can be fatal. It cuts off the flow of the river, backing up the water for miles, causing potential danger to surrounding farms, crops, properties, and cattle.

B. In the Spiritual:

The **Log Jam** happens when we allow the *logs of offense* to pile up and restrict the flow of the Spirit, which results in lack of peace in our lives. It can happen all at once or over time. The scripture tells us in 1 Thessalonians 5, *Quench not the Spirit*. Some versions replace the word *quench* with *grieve*. We grieve God when we allow the logs to pile up and restrict the flow of the Spirit in our lives. By restricting the flow of the Spirit in our lives, we restrict peace and anointing.

All river drivers were watchful and skilled at reading the river, but it was the Elite Jam's job to identify risks and clear obstructions ahead of the logs in order to prevent a jam from happening. At the onset of a wing jam or a center jam, the Elite Jam jumped into action to clear the logs to prevent a pile up. However, the Elite Jam's skilled ability to read the river and *clear the way* was not a new concept. In ancient Near East, "Preparing the way" was synonymous for clearing away obstacles from the road. It was customary to send representatives ahead in preparation for a king's visit.

Malachi 3 says,
Behold, I will send my messenger, and he shall prepare the way before me: and the Lord, whom ye seek, shall suddenly come to his temple...

We know that John the Baptist was the forerunner of Jesus and that he was known for preaching the message "Make straight the way of the Lord." John the Baptist was a river driver. He cleared away religious obstacles and debris by preparing the hearts and the minds of the Jewish people for the coming Messiah.

In Ephesians Paul writes,
Be ye angry, and sin not: let not the sun go down upon your wrath:

Why did Paul write this?

Because he was giving them a new way of thinking. Rather than an eye for an eye and a tooth for a tooth. He was saying forgive quickly, so that the devil doesn't get a foothold.

As a river driver, you need to work hard and fast to clear obstacles and debris that create log jams, so not to obstruct the peace of God in your heart and in your mind.

The LORD said in Isaiah,
Forget the former things; do not dwell on the past. See, I am doing a new thing! Now it springs up; do you not perceive it? I am making a way in the wilderness and streams in the wasteland.[32]

THE PARABLE OF STUCKNESS

Jay Shetty shares this parable about a man who came across a fast-moving river…

> The man knew that if he wanted to get home, he would need to cross the raging river, but though he tried, he couldn't get across on foot. So, he built a raft and placed it in the river and before he could get on it the raft fell apart. So, he built another. He placed the raft in the river and made it safely to the other side.
>
> The raft worked so well the man didn't want to leave it behind, so he tied it to himself. And while on his journey, he came to a thickly wooded forest, one that he would need to pass through to get home. The forest was dense and no matter how hard he tried; he couldn't get through the forest with the raft on his back.
>
> *The man had to decide:* Do I take the raft off and continue or do I stay stuck?

SOMETIMES WE STAY stuck because we haven't let go of something. Is there something you haven't let go of that is keeping you stuck?[33]

The writer of the Gospel of John records these words of Jesus at the Feast of Tabernacles,

If any man thirst, let him come unto me, and drink. He that believeth on me, as the scripture hath said, out of his belly shall flow rivers of living water.

In Revelation 22, John writes about that river again, only this time it's on a universal scale. He wants us to know that the River of Life flows down from the throne of God. The river is the Holy Spirit. It's meant to flow to us and through us and not to be obstructed by bitterness, anger, revenge, or the need to hold a grudge.

*How do you know if you have a **log jam**?*

Well, here's some signs you should watch for:

1) When joy and peace trickle in, rather than flow. 2) When you find yourself consumed with wanting vengeance or justice. 3) When you find yourself constantly criticizing or judging the person(s). 4) When what happened to you is always on your mind. 5) When you see the person and give a quick eye roll. 6) When you ruminate and lose sleep over the injustice.

Why should I care? you ask.

Well, you've heard this already, but the Scripture instructs us to, *Prohibit the Spirit.*

The word quench here, means, *to put out, to put an end to*. Paul tells us to hold fast to that which is good, and he speaks of the Divine presence as a God of Peace—so when negativity builds up, the Spirit can't flow, and when the Spirit can't flow, it quenches peace, and when peace is quenched, it affects you in a big way. Not just internally, but externally—misery loves company!

Because emotions have memory, it's easy to allow the logs to keep us stuck and stranded.

Isaiah writes,
Instead of your shame you will receive a double portion...[34]

The good news is that just like the Canaanite woman, you have the choice to push and steer the logs downstream. In the end, her persistence and hard work paid off when Jesus healed her suffering daughter and restored them to community.

Remember Mephibosheth's name means both *from the mouth of shame*—and—*from the mouth of God.* His story was forward moving and progressive. What began in a barren wasteland, ended in a palace with a seat at the king's table. God will give you a double portion, but you've got to get the logs to the Mill first.

Jesus prayed in the garden of Gethsemane, "Let this cup pass from me," and not long after that, he cried out from the cross, "Father, forgive them; for they know not what they do." He demonstrated that forgiveness wasn't a feeling, but an act of the will.

But shouldn't the offender apologize first? you ask.

No. You don't need the offender's acknowledgment or their apology to move the logs forward. Did the soldiers apologize to Jesus?

But I've tried, and it didn't work. I still feel the same way toward them, you say.

That's okay! It took fifteen hundred years of rolling Israel's sins ahead each year on the Day of Atonement before their sins were ever actually forgiven.

Don't give up. Forgiveness is a process. You might not feel different immediately and that's fine. Stop beating yourself up! In your mind, you've got to picture yourself where you want to be and live there. Abraham was called the father of many nations long before he had a son. And the Scripture tells us that he staggered not at the promise of God through unbelief but was strong in faith giving glory to God.

I wonder how many times in the twenty-five years that Abraham waited for Isaac that he had to remind himself of the promise, before he was ever able to hold it?

Paul writes a lot about Abraham in Romans. In chapter 8, he reminds us that,
All things work together for good to them that love God, to them who are the called according to his purpose.

PANDORA'S BOX

When I was twenty-seven years old, I experienced a new kind of hurt. *Church hurt.* I was a young wife and a mother of three small boys. My husband was over the Children's Church, I was a Sunday school teacher; he was the choir director, I sang in the choir; he was the church carpenter, I was the toilet cleaner; he ushered, I greeted; and together, we directed the annual Easter Cantata. He built the props, I painted them; he played Jesus, I played the woman whose daughter needed a healing, but something happened that year that left me feeling like an empty shell, and that memory goes like this...

OCTOBER 31, 1999, a white car slowly passes by my house. It turns up the next street and circles back around. *It does this several times.*

An hour later, gravel crunches and draws my attention to the white car rolling to a stop in my driveway. I don't recognize the driver or the passenger in the front seat, but when the passenger in the back steps out, *I know her.* Rita is the oldest daughter of one of the lay ministers at my church, and my newly acquired sister-in-law.

Rita knocks on the kitchen door and asks to use the bathroom. Her clothes reek of pot and cigarettes.

"Who's your friends? I've not seen them before. Does Wayne know you're hanging out with them while he's at work?"

She sweeps a strand of hair behind her ear. "Leah and Kayne. You know them. They've come to church with me."

"You mean the Kayne who was in jail?"

She gives a quick eyeroll. "They're just friends," she says, breezing past me.

The bathroom door closes, and the shower turns on. My brow makes a question mark.

The small of my back presses into the kitchen counter as I wait for her to emerge. The shower turns off and the toilet flushes. I cross my arms over my chest. Her tennis shoes squeak on the floor as she makes her way toward me.

She pushes her glasses up and peers over the thin frames. "Did Will go to Tennessee for work like he planned on?"

"Ayuh," I say, in my Maine dialect. "He'll be back Friday night."

"Well, call me if you need anything. Say, what time are you meeting my mom to decorate for the harvest party?"

"As soon as the boys get their shoes on. I've gotta meet the jumpy house guy at 2 o'clock. You wanna help?"

"Have fun with that," she says with a half chuckle.

The door closes.

I stare out the window as the white car backs down the driveway and think nothing more of it until Friday night when my husband returns home from Tennessee, and two church brothers come over for their weekly jam session.

Brother Clay and Brother Aaron arrive and make their way past my husband and me in the kitchen to the music room in the basement, where their band name *39 Stripes* is painted on the cinder block wall.

Seconds later, Brother Clay shouts, "Hey! Did someone borrow my equipment?"

I shake my head.

My husband responds with a mouth full of brownie. "No. Why?"

Footsteps thunder up the stairs. First, Brother Clay, then Brother Aaron. Hands spinning like helicopter blades.

"Everything's gone! My bass and bass amp, his keyboard, your electric guitar, the acoustic guitar..."

"You can't be serious!" my husband says.

A dry heat sweeps my face as I reach down and slide the stuffed shells out of the oven.

"Babe, anyone been here while I was gone?"

It's no longer the heat from the oven I feel, but the three sets of eyes boring holes in me like lasers.

"Just Rita," I say. *Just Rita! The one who had served time for stealing a dead woman's checks!*

Now it makes sense, the white car circling my house, the shower turning on, Rita confirming that my husband had gone out of town and my plans to leave the house to decorate the church for the harvest party. I kick the oven door shut and set the shells on the hotplate in center of the table. "It was Rita! She was acting strange!"

My husband let's out a strangled yelp. "Call the police. We've been robbed!"

I throw the oven mitts off and dial 9-1-1. Afterward, my husband calls the pastor. The more he tells him about the robbery, the louder the pastor gets. We can tell the pastor's mad, but not at Rita, at us for calling the police.

I gnaw on my fingernails and stare at the steam rising from the stuffed shells in the center of the table.

"What do you mean, come to your house *tonight* for an emergency meeting? It's after nine o'clock! You should be coming over here! It was my house that got robbed, not yours—

My husband paces the length of the kitchen, all twelve feet of it. His steel-toed boots clomp back and forth over the shiny linoleum. He grips the phone, and his knuckles turn whiter than a garden full of Peonies. "What do you mean, don't file a police report? I have to if we want to get our stuff back."

I gulp.

Brother Clay's brow slowly rises like a periscope in enemy waters and Brother Aaron runs his hands up through his hairline, keeping them there.

My husband inhales. He clenches his teeth to keep in the breath, and when he finally exhales, it sounds like a balloon deflating.

His mouth twists with his words. "But pastor why are we being punished? Why are we being made to be the bad guys?"

The pastor's voice trumpets through the phone. "Brother Will, I forbid you from filing a police report and if the four of you don't show up tonight for the meeting, you'll be removed from your ministries and sat down for six months!"

"B-b-but Pastor, how will we get our stuff back?"

"You won't!" he says matter-of-factly.

I shake my head hard and fast. *Don't say anything else! You know what can happen if we disobey!*

I think about Jonah's disobedience. Families have been kicked out of the church for less than this. *I don't want that to be us! What will our boys do? All their friends go there.*

My husband stomps his boot one time, then two, breaking the silence. "You can't do that! We didn't do anything wrong."

"I can, and I will! Your wife's vindictive. She's got a grudge against Rita. Rita deserves a second chance."

"Who me?" I say, pointing to myself.

My husband let's out a gasp. "You can't be serious! My wife doesn't have a grudge against Rita or anyone. She's one of the kindest people I know. She's given Rita plenty of second chances, and thirds, and fourths, the whole church has. If Rita didn't do it, then she doesn't have anything to worry about now does she?"

"Brother Will, the ministers will be here in an hour and if the four of you aren't present for the meeting, there will be consequences to pay."

The call ends, and there is a long pause, followed by lights. Bright flashing ones.

Two officers step out onto the gravel. One walks around the exterior of the house with a flashlight, the other approaches the walkway. A knot forms in my stomach. My eyes make a silent plea. *What do I tell them?*

My husband motions for a huddle. Brother Clay and Brother Aaron move in closer until touching shoulders.

"Listen guys, we all know what will happen if we disobey, so if I can't get your stuff back without having to file a report, I'll give you the cash. It happened at my house. I'm responsible. Deal?"

"Deal," they say as three sharp knocks send fear surging through my veins.

My hands tremble as I answer the door. "Come in," I say.

The officer stands in front of the baker's rack with his feet apart. His eyes bounce from Brother Clay to Brother Aaron to my husband to the stuffed shells to the salad to the rolls to the brownies to the stack of clean plates with the napkins folded neatly beside them and to our three boys who poke their heads around the corner with wide worried eyes.

I chew my bottom lip and focus on the one brownie missing from the pan. Our Friday night breaking bread together has forever changed.

50

"Look," my husband says to the officer, "all we want to know is if we can get our stuff back without filing a police report?"

The officer flips open a small notepad. "Don't you want to put the person in jail who did this?"

Put them under the jail would be more like it, I tell myself. "No, we can't! You wouldn't understand. Can you just check the pawn shops to see if they have our stuff?" I say.

"It wouldn't do any good. They're not gonna' give you the stuff back without a police report. Why? Do you know who did it?"

My eyes drop.

The officer shakes his head. "See! This is what happens. You don't file a police report and the next person they rob isn't so—"

The door opens and in rushes Wayne and Rita.

"Who are you?" The officer asks.

"His little brother. We were on our way home and saw the lights. Everything okay?"

"They were robbed," the officer says.

Wayne's neck snaps back with surprise.

I cross my arms and rake my glance past Wayne to Rita. "But you probably knew that?" I say.

Rita tosses her hands in the air and erupts into tears. "Francine, I can't believe you think I did it. Do you think that, Will?"

A pause fills the room.

"Willie, how could you, man!" Wayne snatches Rita's hand. "Come on, honey, let's go home!"

The door slams.

Red taillights speed up the hill and disappear.

"Maybe we were wrong. Maybe she didn't do it," Brother Clay says.

"If she is guilty, then she deserves an Oscar," my husband says. "Her performance was, let's just say, believable."

Brother Aaron nods.

My eyes water and I taste the salt of the tears at the back of my throat. "I know what my gut is telling me. She did it and now she's going to get away with it."

That evening, I toss and turn in my bed and can't get Rita off my mind. I want her to tell the truth. I want the pastor to know I'm a good person. I want my brother-in-law to know I didn't make it up. I want our stuff back and the twelve hundred dollars we gave Brother Clay and Brother Aaron.

It's not fair! I bawl my fists beneath the blankets and tense up like a baby with colic. I haven't felt this kind of anger and injustice since I was a little girl, when all I wanted was for my uncle to tell the truth, and for my aunt to believe me.

My eyes water again as I stare at my husband's long back and wonder how he does it. *How he can sleep at a time like this?* The pastor's words, the white car, and Rita's suspicious behavior pile up in my thoughts and in my fists, only to empty out in my tears.

I roll over the other way, taking the blankets with me. Snot mixes with tears and I clench my teeth. *I hate her!*

Suddenly, the sound of metal-on-metal sends shivers through my spine and up into my hairline. Red brake lights flash, then stop, flash, then stop. *They're back!*

My heart pounds. I try to roll over, to sit up, to move, to call my husband's name, but nothing works, except for my eyeballs, they rotate in their sockets, like when I was a little girl, when night terrors weren't quarantined to sleep, and when monsters, both real and imagined, chased me.

As soon as I'm able, I throw the blankets off and zip through the darkness like a field mouse, checking the locks on the windows and doors, and when I don't see anything, but an old green taxi in the street, I sigh with relief. *I'm not a little girl anymore! I'm a wife! A mom!* I tell myself, but this reminder comes too little, too late. Pandora's box is open, I can't close it, and from it comes all the things I wish to forget.

Back in bed, I pull the blankets around me in hopes that when I wake up, all the fear and anger and injustices will be back in the box where they belong.

I breathe deep and exhale. Breathe deep again, and exhale. *I'm fine*, I tell myself. But, *Am I really?* I don't feel fine. I feel like *that* little girl.

My head sinks into the pillow, and when I can no longer fight sleep, it yanks me from my bed in Virginia to the little brown house with the mustard-trimmed door at night, lying on the top bunk with Patches our family cat at my feet and Buster my stuffed dog under my arm, where fear and anger and injustice stems, back to where it all began, back to the land of Canaan, Maine. (An excerpt from my memoir coming soon, titled *In the Land of Canaan: A Little Girl's Giants*).[35]

SUDDENLY, I WAS set on revenge, I was harboring unforgiveness, and I felt justified in doing so. *Rita was my enemy!* You know what you do when you have an enemy, right?

…You pray against them, of course! You don't bless them.

…You hate them. You get even with them.

All of which raises the question:

What would Jonah do?

Breaking up a wing jam before it becomes a log jam

Photo credit: West Branch Historical Preservation Committee,
http://themaineboomhouses.org/photos-from-the-past/

4

JONAH & THE LOG JAM

"We must develop and maintain the capacity to forgive. He who is devoid of the power to forgive is devoid of the power to love. There is some good in the worst of us and some evil in the best of us. When we discover this, we are less prone to hate our enemies"

— Martin Luther King, Jr.

DID JONAH DIE
when
the
sailors
threw
him
overboard,
or
did he pull a Bear Grylls and find an air pocket, eat sushi, and chug seaweed shakes for three days and nights while waiting for extraction?

Honestly, it would make better sense that he died, and here's why. The Scripture teaches that except a corn of wheat falls to the ground and die, it abides alone: but if it die, it brings forth much fruit.

What if the miracle of Jonah wasn't that he lived? What if the miracle was that he died and was resurrected?

What do you mean?!

Relax. Jonah dying doesn't change the Good News in any way.

Years ago, my husband put on a long robe with a belt he made from twine, draped a fishing net around his shoulders and hung *real* crawfish and Alaskan crab legs and scaly stinky fish all over it, then walked out onto the stage and with an English accent narrated the story as if he was Jonah from within the fish's belly.

The kids were amazed.

The adults were mesmerized.

It was awesome!

Historians, theologians, and even artists have long been captivated by the narrative contained within the four chapters.

Sadly, until the past few years, I didn't know the book of Jonah was more than a book about what happens when you disobey God and His *man* in charge down here, i.e. the pastor.

The theme of Jonah isn't *see-I-told-you-so* like I was conditioned to believe. It was a question God had for Jonah that *really* was a question for Israel that is really a question for us today:

Can you forgive your worst enemy?

We will delve deeper into the forgiveness part in a minute, but first we need to talk about the whole whale thing.

What if it was a corpse the whale had vomited up on the seashore?

Really though…what if?

It's possible!

Here's a line from Jonah 2:
*I cried by reason of mine affliction unto the LORD, and he heard me; out of the belly of **hell** cried I, and thou heardest my voice.*

The word "hell" in the original Hebrew is the word *Sheol.* In the Greek it is the word, Hades. Either way, it means the place of the dead or where the dead go when the soul separates from the body.[36] Both good and bad, rich and poor, young and old, male and female are believed to go there. Perhaps, this is what Jesus meant when He told the parable about Abraham's Bosom or what 1 Peter 3 means, when it says that Jesus went and preached to the spirits in prison after His death and before His resurrection. The Jews believe that from *Sheol,* the dead can communicate with the living and the living with the dead. Like in the Jewish movie *Loving Leah.* Certain Jewish sects also believe that the spirit hovers over the body for three days with the possibility of it reentering.

Then three verses later, Jonah prays:
*I went down to the bottoms of the mountains; the earth with her bars was about me for ever: yet thou has brought up my life from **corruption**, O LORD my God.*

The word "corruption" also means "pit," otherwise called, the "bottomless pit." Both "pit" and "bottomless pit" are words used to describe hell. Thus, reinforcing that he may have died and was in *Sheol.* Here's an example from the New Testament where the Apostle Peter quotes King David, saying, *Because thou wilt not leave my soul in hell, neither wilt thou suffer thine Holy One to see corruption.* In other words, God is not going to leave David in *Sheol,* neither will he suffer the Holy One to see decay.

Then, the very next verse in Jonah says:
*When my soul **fainted** within me I remembered the LORD: and my prayer came in unto thee, into thine holy temple.*

The word "soul" in Hebrew is the word *nefesh,* which means "life."[37] What if Jonah's life expired? The word 'fainted' here in the Hebrew means "to turn" or "to turn and cover." Keeping in mind that the Jews read the story of Jonah every year on the Day of Atonement, which is called in Hebrew, Yom Kippur, and means 'to cover.' The Jews also believe that if someone violates a law it is punishable by death and can only be atoned for through the death of that person. We'll talk more about that later. But for now, back to atonement. Atonement is the covering up of sin. It is the rolling ahead of their sins from God's sight until the next Day of Atonement.

Now skip down to the first two verses of chapter 3:
*And the word of the LORD came unto Jonah the second time, saying, **Arise**, go to Nineveh, that great city, and preach unto it the preaching that I bid thee.*

The word "arise" is the same word "cum or cumi" that Jesus used when He took the dead girl by the hand and said unto her, *Talitha cumi.*[38]

In other words, Jesus told the girl that had been dead to get up!

Here's what Jesus had to say in Matthew:
For as Jonah was three days and three nights in the whale's belly; so shall the son of man be three days and three nights in the heart of the earth.

The words of Jesus in Matthew would make more sense to a Jewish audience if Jonah died. The miraculous sign in the book of Jonah was the resurrection of Jonah, which was why when Jesus was asked for a sign that He was the Savior, He gave them Jonah.

John 2 lets us know that it wasn't until after the resurrection of Jesus that His disciples remembered His words and believed the Scripture, that He would rise from the grave on the third day, so that Scripture could be fulfilled.

Wait!—what Scripture?

No such reference in the Old Testament immediately comes to mind. Nowhere does it tell us that the Son of Man would spend three days and three nights in the heart of the earth, and on the third day rise from the dead. Nowhere, unless of course, you are reading the story of Jonah.

Which brings me back to the question, Did Jonah die when the sailors threw him overboard, or did he pull a Bear Grylls and find an air pocket, eat sushi, and chug seaweed shakes three days and nights while waiting for extraction?

Just one more thing.

In Matthew 16, where Jesus asks His disciples, "Who do you say that I am," and Simon Peter says, "You are the Christ the Son of the Living God," and Jesus says, "Blessed are you Simon Bar-Jonah for flesh and blood hath not revealed it to thee…"

There are two things I find interesting. The first is that Peter recognizes Jesus as the Living God before he was crucified, buried, and raised from the dead. The second is that Jesus calls him Bar-Jonah. Transliteration infers Jonah as "Yonah" which refers to a prophetic voice and "bar" which means "son of." Jesus is telling

Simon Peter that he is a prophetic voice that is announcing Jesus as the Living God who would raise from the dead just like Jonah.

The Old Testament is the schoolmaster that brings us to Christ. Jonah died and was resurrected so that Nineveh could live. Jesus died and was resurrected so that *all* could live.

Up until recently, I didn't know the book of Jonah was more than a book about what happens when you disobey God.

The theme of Jonah isn't *see-I-told-you-so* like I thought. Rather, it was a question God had for Jonah that really was a question for Israel that is really a question for us today:

Can you forgive your worst enemy?[39]

We first meet Jonah in 2 Kings 14, where he is called to be a prophet and sent by the LORD to Jeroboam the king of Israel, who was an evil king. The LORD wanted Jonah to go to Jeroboam and tell him that He was going to bless him and expand his kingdom.

So, Jonah obeys. He goes to the king. The LORD blesses the king. And the king gets worse!

Now fast forward to the book of Jonah.

The LORD tells the prophet to go to the great city of Nineveh and preach to the people there that they should repent or else they will be destroyed, but this time, Jonah doesn't obey, instead, he flees to Joppa, where he buys a one-way-ticket to Tarshish, 2500 miles in the opposite direction.

To understand why Jonah does this, we first need to understand the Neo-Assyrian Empire that haunts the backdrop of the Jonah story.

The Assyrians were the superpower of the day—not just of that day, but, for hundreds of years. Historians record that the Assyrian armies used barbaric methods to torture their captives and were known for their siege warfare. This included the deportation of the ten tribes of the northern kingdom of Israel, where Jonah lived, to Assyria,

a foreign land,

with foreign food,

and language,

and people,

and gods.

The Assyrians inflicted cruel and unusual punishments on their captives like burying them up to their necks in the desert and cutting out their tongues, so that they couldn't swallow. Never mind the glaring fact that Nineveh is the capital of Assyria according to the Hebrew Scriptures.

The Assyrians treated Israel horribly! They were the enemy of the Jews.

Of course, Jonah didn't want to go!

You wouldn't either!

Perhaps, in the recesses of Jonah's mind was the question, "What if God shows the Assyrians kindness and they get worse, *way worse*, like king Jeroboam?"

In case you are still unclear as to how cruel the Assyrians were, here's an inscription from an Assyrian temple that records the words of king Ashurbanipal about the physical punishment he inflicted on his captives:

"I built a pillar at the city gate and I flayed all the chief men who had revolted, and I covered the pillar with their skins; some I walled up inside the pillar, some I impaled upon stakes."[40]

That is why Jonah refused to go.

That is why he fled.

That is why he was fast asleep in the bottom of a boat bound for southern Spain.

That is why a terrifying storm arose nearly breaking the boat apart.

That is why he was thrown overboard.

That is why he was swallowed by a giant fish in the middle of the Mediterranean Sea and spit out three days later.

So, back to God's question for Jonah that was really a question for Israel that is really a question for us today,

Can you forgive those who hurt you?

It's a real question.

Jonah struggled with forgiveness. *Do you?*

Jonah who had been vomited up only days earlier, reluctantly announced to Nineveh that in forty days their city would be destroyed.

Why does Jonah care about Nineveh?

Oh, that's right!—He doesn't!

Jonah hates the Assyrians!

He doesn't want them to repent. He wants them to die!

"Hurt people hurt people," Charles Eads said. We want our enemies to pay. We want our enemies to hurt, because we hurt.

Jonah wanted the Assyrians to suffer because of the pain they inflicted on his people. But that's not what happened in the story. Nineveh repented, and God changed His mind, Jonah didn't change his mind. He still wanted God to judge them and to bring justice for Israel. Without judgment, there could be no justice. At least, that's what Jonah thought. What he failed to realize was that justice and restitution could never give him back what he lost.

In chapter 4, Jonah tells God,
I knew thou art a gracious God, and merciful, slow to anger, and of great kindness...

What Jonah was really saying was,
See, I knew You wouldn't do it! I knew You would have a change of heart!

Jonah seeing his enemy blessed infuriated him. Have you ever felt that way?

I know I have.

While growing up, not only did my uncle sexually abuse me, he abused my older sister Pauline, too, and sold us to other men. He killed our pet rabbit and told us that if we ever told, he would kill us like he did the rabbit. He terrified, terrorized, and gave us nightmares. Whenever we heard the extended family praising him and calling him the "World's best Uncle," and saying, "He'll make a great father one day," we became frustrated with "What about me?" and "Look what a monster he is."

Putting myself in Jonah's sandals—I could see why he was angry that the LORD extended the same grace and mercy to his enemy as He had to his people. Jonah would rather die, than see his enemies blessed.

The problem is that anger leads to bitterness that leads to resentment that leads to log jams...

IN 2006, I was at FunQuest with my boys, and while they roller skated, I sat in a two-seater booth with my Bible. The place was noisy and packed.

As I read from the Gospel of John, I heard a voice and looked up to see an elderly African American woman with her hand on the empty seat across from me. "Is this seat taken? It's the only one left," she said.

I slid my Bible out of the way and moved my boy's stuff to make room for her.

"I'm eighty-seven," she said, "I can't hardly stand to be on my feet anymore," she added as she sat down. She looked at the upside-down page I was on and asked if that was the book of John I was reading from.

I smiled wide.

"That's one of my favorite books," she said as she slid her legs under the table. Her knees bumped mine.

"I can see why...It's one of my favorites, too! I love how John expresses the dual nature of Christ. He was all God and all man at the same time—the God-Man."

"I never actually thought of it like that," she said, and then added, "the God-Man—I like that."

"Can I tell you something?" I said with a giggle. "I love the book of Romans and Acts, too. Do you know the book of Acts is the only book in the New Testament that doesn't end with the word *amen*?" I said to her.

"No, I didn't know. Why do you suppose that is?"

"That's because it's still for us today," I partly shouted, and partly spoke.

She leaned forward and peered over her thick frames at me. "Can I tell you something?"

"Of course—" I leaned happily forward to hear her over the song *put your left skate in, put your left skate out, put your left skate in and shake it all about* music playing on the loudspeakers.

She paused. Her eyes darted from the bright blue wall with neon paint to the kids doing the Hokey Pokey to the long concession line and then back to me.

While I waited for the *something* she had to say, I anticipated what Bible passage she would bring up, which verse we would discuss next—*The woman at the well* or *wives submit yourselves to your husbands* or *women shouldn't wear that which pertains to a man* or *women keep silence in the church...*

"I hate white people," she said with a loud whisper.

Wait!—What?!

My neck jerked back. I could feel the skin between my eyes as it wrinkled.

Did she say, I hate white people? All white people? Even a Yankee like me? I'm from Maine! What did I do?

Her eyes welled and she stared down at her hands that were cupped on the Formica tabletop.

IN THAT MOMENT, the things Mr. V taught me in history class and the things I'd read flashed through my head:

The Jim Crow South,

The Separate but Equal legal doctrine in the constitutional law,

The Confederate battle flag,

The Tuskegee Experiment,

The black-and-white water fountains,
Harriet Tubman,
Fredrick Douglass,
Nat Turner,
Rosa Parks,
Dr. Martin Luther King, Jr.,
and other haunting images of people of color, men, women, and children, being kicked to the ground and beaten with clubs, imprisoned, attacked by dogs, spat upon, sprayed with fire hoses, tortured, terrorized, and tear gassed—all because they wanted the right to vote. *They deserved the right to vote.*

I aced my eleventh-grade history final exam and even got the bonus questions right, but nothing prepared me in the North for that moment in the South, when I would sit across from an elderly woman of color in a crowded roller skate rink as she mustered up the courage to say, *I hate white people!*

But who could blame her, right?

Her words were a cry for help! The question was,

How would I respond?

Even now as I write this, I am reminded of the police officer kneeling with his knee on George Floyd's neck as he lay dying, and the cruel backdrop this country has of slavery, oppression, hatred, and bigotry, which haunts us like the Neo-Assyrian backdrop of Jonah's day.

Recently, my close friend, Lisa, who is a person of color, and I were discussing White Privilege and what it means to each of us. My definition and hers differed entirely.

I said to my friend, "I didn't experience any advantages of being white while growing up. I grew up poor! I went to the bathroom on five-gallon buckets until I was in eleventh grade and drew water from a rusty brown hand-pump outside. I wore hand-me-downs. I was ridiculed and bullied throughout school. I was in Title-1 enrichment classes through the eighth grade. I was a food stamp recipient. Not you, you had nice things, nice clothes, a nice car, a big house, you excelled in school...not me...I was what people considered, *Poor white trash*."

To which my friend said, "That's not white privilege." Then she added. "No matter how rich we are or how much fame we have or how educated we are or how successful we become, a person of color will always be below the poorest white person."

I felt a sinking feeling in my gut as I could suddenly see how a person of color might feel, it's only freedom if you're holding the cards. To all those who aren't holding the cards—it doesn't feel like freedom. *Although much progress has been made.*

NOW BACK TO the *I hate white people*. The words had barely left her lips when I reached my hands across the table and held hers. They were soft and delicate, and shaking.

"I'm sorry!" I said, which caused her to look up. "I'm sorry for all the horrible things we did to you—for all of the times we mistreated you, cursed at you, made you suffer, caused you to feel inferior and afraid. I'm sorry for all of it! I can't say, I know how you feel, but I can say, I've suffered too—I can say, I know what pain is—I can say, I know what it is to hold a grudge and to hate someone because they hurt you...I was sexually abused and raped as a child—I know it's not the same, but the hate is the same, the pain is the same!"

The woman and I, though poles apart in age and from very different backgrounds sat *shiva* in a little booth in the middle of a noisy roller rink. And the same time, we sat *shiva* at the foot of the cross, where the ground is even, where there is no racial divide, no white or black, no Jew or gentile, no male or female, where we are *all* one and the same because of the Suffering One, who's blood was applied to the universal doorpost.

Suffering unites humanity. It has a way of blurring the lines and bringing the Holy down. God sat *shiva* with us then, just as He did on the front row at Dirigo Girl's State, just as He does now in the middle of Me-Too movements and Black Lives Matter. *God is love and forgiveness is the ultimate act of love.*

I can take you to the very spot at the skate rink, where we sat and held hands and cried, to the table where I used the peavey hook to turn the *logs* over and to see it through the eyes—the eyes of an eighty-seven-year-old-woman-of-color raised in the deep south. The booth where two river drivers with pickaroon poles steered the *logs* of hate and the decades of pain in a forward motion downstream together.

So back to God's question for Jonah that was really a question for Israel that is really a question for us today,

Can you forgive your worst enemy?

It's a real question for hurting people in stuck places.

Jonah who had been vomited up *only* days earlier went to Nineveh and reluctantly announced that in forty days their city would be destroyed if they didn't repent.

He doesn't want them to repent. He wants fire and brimstone to rain down upon their heads!

Kind of what I wanted to happen to Rita when she robbed my house and to my uncle when he robbed my innocence.

I wanted to be vindicated, which was what Jonah wanted, and what the woman at the roller skate rink wanted, and what I wanted when I saw people praising my uncle. Vindication is what you want when you have unresolved forgiveness. It's the "We want our enemies to hurt, because we hurt" thing.

For the longest time, seeing my uncle on a pedestal was a hard pill to swallow for me and my sisters.

Harder than a whale swallowing a man?
Yes!

The Apostle Paul wrote to the church at Rome these words, *Therefore if thine enemy hunger, feed him; if he thirst, give him drink; for in so doing thou shalt heap coals of fire on his head.*

Paul gave the church a new way of conquering the enemy by telling them to be kind.

But what if they don't deserve it?

My question then is, Did the Roman soldiers deserve it? Did the people mocking Jesus deserve it? Did the ones who secretly betrayed Jesus deserve it?

According to Divine forgiveness, yes.

What Paul is essentially saying is that every time you are kind to those who hurt you, you are moving logs downstream. With the downstream motion comes the new life. It frees you from the resentment and bitterness that causes log jams and keeps you stuck. It's what being a river driver is all about. It's pushing the hard feelings downstream long enough to come to the place of completion. A place where God can use what the enemy intended for your harm to bless you. It's taking up your cross daily, or should I say, "Pickaroon pole daily." Believe me, your flesh may not feel like it, but when the logs reach the Mill, you'll be glad you put in the work.

Paul wrote in Ephesians 4,
And be ye kind one to another, tenderhearted, forgiving one another, even as God for Christ's sake hath forgiven you.

In the sermon on the mount, Jesus said,
Love your enemies, bless them that curse you, do good to them that hate you, and pray for them which despitefully use you, and persecute you.

Which brings me back to the opening salvo,

Did Jonah die when the sailors threw him overboard, or did he pull a Bear Grylls and find an air pocket, eat sushi, and chug seaweed shakes three days and nights while waiting for extraction?

I have a sneaking suspicion Jonah died. For something new to grow, something has to die.

Log boom being towed across the lake

Photo credit: West Branch Historical Preservation Committee,
http://themaineboomhouses.org/photos-from-the-past/

5

ASH POLES & LOG BOOMS

"Unforgiveness is when you freeze-frame someone in their weakness"
— Mike Meadows

AFTER RITA ROBBED my house, the first time my uncle hurt me came back with a rush…

Uncle Jerry calls out, "Count me in. I pick Francine!"
The florescent light flickers as he scrolls the dented garage door down. The undersized wheels squeal on the track.
I look up, way up, past his beer belly to his three-day old whiskers.
It's me, David, and him, Goliath. I'm dizzy, and clammy, and shaky. The extra attention he gives me causes my belly to fill with collywobbles.
His mechanic hands sweep me up. I'm jolted into the air and land on his back with a thud. He "neighs" and rakes his boot through the grass as if it's a hoof, and gallops excitedly around grandpa's tow truck with Dodge's Auto Salvage painted on the sides. He races past the twenty-one

cousins lined up against the tarpapered garage wall, half shoeless, half shirtless, waiting on hide and seek to begin.

The cousins chant. "Francine's Uncle Jerry's pet!"

I'm not his pet! I secure my puffball and hug his neck to keep from bouncing off.

Richard, the oldest cousin, begins to count: "One Mississippi, two Mississippi, three Mississippi…"

The cousins scatter.

The horse neighs, rakes its hoof through the grass one more time, and takes off like the Kentucky derby, past the trail of parked cars, behind the unused portion of grandma's house, where it halts.

No longer the horse, he lays me down beside the forsaken septic mound and pushes me backward, squishing my prized puffball. Slivers of slate and sharp pebbles pierce my elbows and tailbone.

"That hurts!"

"Sh-h. Uncle Jerry loves you. Not a sound."

His sandpaper hand holds my face down and covers my mouth and nose. *I can't breathe!* The same way I couldn't, when a Fire Ball lodged in my throat, and before Mom freed it with her finger.

"Don't think about telling anyone. Not even Richard. I'll kill you." His head signifies what my answer should be. "This is our little secret."

I nod. In the distance, I hear "Ninety-seven Mississippi, ninety-eight Mississippi, ninety-nine Mississippi, one-hundred. Ready or not here I come!"

Uncle Jerry shushes my cries and removes his hand. A feather-like touch sweeps across my belly button. The sound of my zipper breaks the silence and with a second feather-like brush my shorts slide off. He yanks my white underwear with pink flowers down. "We don't tell secrets. Ayuh?" His voice is as steel.

I shake my head. *Yes. No. I don't know.*

My muscles stiffen and lungs slow. *Am I breathing?* My mind commands me to move—to get up—to run, but I'm unable to respond.

He yanks my tube-top up and rubs his scruff on my breastbone, the weight of his chest crushes me.

My pinky won't budge to squash the tiny insects with the siphons buzzing around my head. I roll my eyes to spin over. But I'm stuck. His body lays across me like the lid on a coffin. The stench of sweat, motor oil, and beer burn my nostrils and eyes. He kisses my mouth. I seal my lips tight.

I yell words in my head, but fear blocks their passage. A second and third mosquito sups. *Why can't I move?*

Tangled in fear, tears seep from my eyes and fill my ear holes.

He sits up on his knees. I silently celebrate and wait for him to leave. Instead, his hips wiggle until his pants hug his kneecaps. His hips jerk forward. The shock so deep and painful my insides twist and turn like a murmuration of black birds. *This isn't Mr. Tickle anymore.*

A scream erupts in my throat but can't escape with his hand locking it in. The pain rips through me—I'd rather suffer a thousand broken legs than one more minute of this.

Tears spill from my eyes and ripple down my cheeks. Moans and gargles escape his mouth.

A stick snaps nearby, and Richard calls out, "Francine, Uncle Jerry, come out, come out, wherever you are."

Uncle Jerry presses his hand to my mouth. "You say a word and I'll kill you."

The footsteps draw closer. "Come out—come out— wherever you are."

Uncle Jerry squeezes my lips forcing them into a fish face. His eyes narrow. "Don't make a sound." The Man in the Moon reflects in the sweat of his brow. A bead of salty water splashes my skin as Richard's footsteps taper away.

Wait! Come back!

My lips sting. "Uncle Jerry loves you. You know that, ayuh?"

I blink twice.

He releases my mouth and pats my head before reaching into his pocket. "This is for being a good little girl." Two dimes and a nickel drop in my hand.

Drunken laughter roars from the oval poker table. "Royal flush!" Grandpa yells.

The clanging of chips comforts me. I picture Grandpa in his blue mechanic shirt with *Dodge's Auto Salvage* embroidered above the pocket and a pack of smokes in it. He sips a beer with a tri-union of cancer-sticks by his elbow—a cigar, a pipe, and a smoldering cigarette.

But now I'm back and gravel digs into my tailbone. Uncle Jerry zips his zipper and jogs away. I place my ear against the ground and monitor the vibrations of his footsteps as he leaves.

The hinges on the screen door creak and Grandpa calls out. "Deal you in, Jerry?"

"Ah nope, Pop, I have an engine to finish. I'm just getting a brewsky."

The hinges creak again, and I lay stock still until the florescent light from the tarpapered garage glows. Relief from the light pacifies me and I exhale the breath I did not know I held. A shadowy image flashes by the curtain-less windows and I shield my eyes from the ghost that haunts the house. Fearful the headless doohickey or the glowing pig's eyes will appear.

I sweep the ground for my underwear and stuff them in my pocket. Sticky goo trickles down my legs and with slow small steps, I make my way past the oval poker table and into the bathroom.

The light comes on and there is blood, so much blood. *I'm going to die. I need help. I can't tell.* I place the small of my back against the wall and slide into a seated position on the floor between the toilet and wicker-waste-basket.

I cover my mouth with both hands and scream. All that comes out is a silent squeal. (An excerpt from my memoir: *In the Land of Canaan: A Little Girl's Giants*).[41]

ONE MOMENT I'M a wife and a mother; the next, a scared little girl. Like a cosmic crash, the trauma of my past collided with the trauma of my present. For the next five months, with no proof other than a hunch to go on, I was consumed with proving Rita robbed me. Every morning, *Rita* was the first thing on my mind, and every evening, *she* was the last. I would lay in bed for hours thinking of ways to coax her into telling the truth. I wanted justice—I wanted vindication—I wanted the church to know I was a good person—I wanted Rita to apologize—I wanted the twelve hundred dollars and all my stuff back! Every time I saw her or heard her name, I remembered the *offense,* and hated her all the more. I became a prisoner in my mind and in my heart. The *sun* had gone down, and the long shadow of hate and bitterness had cast its darkness upon me.

Unforgiveness is when you freeze-frame someone in their weakness. I had freeze-framed Rita in her weakness, and in doing so, I had freeze-framed myself. This makes me think of something Pete Rollins said: "Trauma steps out of time and until you heal from the trauma, time can't start back up."

Pete's words ring true. Every morning, after my husband would leave for work, and every evening, after he would fall asleep, I would walk the floors. Making almost hourly rounds, checking and rechecking the doors and windows to make sure they were locked, and tightening the blinds to ensure no burglars could see in. When I would finally fall asleep, the slightest noise would cause me to freeze with fear—car alarms, sticks snapping, brakes scraping, rain falling, tree branches scratching the house. My heart would pound out of my chest and I would lay there paralyzed with only my eyes able to move. To top it off, I was terrified of going down to the basement to wash clothes. I was convinced an intruder would jump out from under the staircase, grab my leg, and yank me down the steps and rape me. I was ashamed of my feelings and afraid of what others in the church would think of me, if they found out, so for months, I kept the secret and suffered in silence.

The pickaroon pole, which was what the river driver used to push and steer logs downstream was up to fourteen feet in length and was made from ash wood. Ash was a flexible wood that would bend to prevent the pole from breaking. Unlike the pickaroon pole, I was inflexible to the point of breaking, when I finally confessed to my friend Donna about the many sleepless nights.

The *wing jam* (also called the right jam) quickly became a log jam, and the more I thought about the injustice of it all, the higher and wider and further backed up the logs became. The robbery caused all the fear and pain and anger of my childhood, which I had stuffed way down deep inside to spring forth like a Jack-in-the-box, and before I knew it, my need for justice had caused me
to
lose
my
peace,
my
joy,
and
my
anointing.

Bitterness led to resentment that led to unforgiveness that led to me praying prayers like "Get her God," "Vengeance is mine saith the Lord," "Touch not mine anointed," and "You reap what you sow."

I was set on revenge. I was determined to prove I was right. I was cultivating the offense as if it were in a petri dish.

In the story of Jonah, the people of Nineveh put on sackcloth and ashes as an outward display of repentance. *They even put it on their cattle!* I wanted Rita to put on sackcloth and ashes and prance around the church to show she was sorry.

Rita had become my enemy and like Jonah, I didn't want God to show the enemy mercy—I was tired of seeing her play the role of the "wrongly accused" at church.
I wanted justice–
I wanted to get even–
I wanted Rita to suffer–
I wanted the church to be mad at her–
I wanted my brother-in-law to know I didn't make it up–
I wanted the pastor to know he had a hypocrite in the choir–

My unwillingness to forgive Rita wasn't *just* about my house being robbed. I was nursing unhealed wounds and I didn't even know it.

The question became,

Can I forgive her?

River drivers and their cork boots

Photo credit: West Branch Historical Preservation Committee,
http://themaineboomhouses.org/photos-from-the-past/

6

A LION IN CORK BOOTS

"Many promising reconciliations have broken down because while both parties come prepared to forgive, neither party come prepared to be forgiven"
— Charles Williams

FOR THE RIVER driver, a log run wasn't always fast flowing water with rushing and bucking logs. Sometimes it was calm stretches, where they could be seen standing up and balancing on logs with their pickaroon poles in hand while floating downstream. River drivers depended heavily upon their cork boots to keep them safe, especially while balancing, running, and jumping over slippery logs up to 13-foot in length. *They never wanted to slip!* One slip could get a limb pinched off between logs and could mean the difference between life and death. The cork boots were boots with thick leather soles. The bottoms were equipped with long spikes for traction. River drivers were quick footed and agile. The cork boots helped them stand firm on floating wet logs and secure their footing.

The apostle Paul tells us to put on the whole armor of God and on numerous occasions draws our attention to the *feet* in his writings.

In the book of Ephesians 6, he writes,

Having your feet shod with the preparation of the gospel of peace;

In Romans 10, he writes,
How beautiful are the feet of them that preach the gospel of peace and bring glad tidings of good things!

But in Romans 3, he switches it up and writes,
Their feet are swift to shed blood:

Paul is telling the saints that there are two kinds of footwear—those of chaos and those of peace. He's encouraging the saints to choose peace in order to stand against the wiles of the devil.

WHAT IS RECONCILIATION?

In Ephesians 2, Paul writes,
But now in Christ Jesus ye who sometimes were far off are made nigh by the blood of Christ. For he is our peace, who hath made both one, and hath broken down the middle wall of partition between us;

According to Vine's Greek New Testament Dictionary, "the word reconciliation comes from the Greek family of words that has its roots in *allasso*. The meaning common to this group of words is "change," "exchange," or "together." One meaning that also has its roots in this Greek family of words is "sun," which comes from the Greek word *sunallasso*."[43]

Reconciliation is a change in relationship and involves a minimum of two people or two groups. Reconciliation is often what moves us from darkness back to light.

Which is why Paul writes in Ephesians, "Be ye angry, and sin not: let not the *sun* go down upon your wrath." The sin he is speaking of has to do with the breakdown of harmony and fellowship. In other words, Paul is saying, reconcile with your brother or sister quickly to restore the bond of peace, so that darkness doesn't cast its long shadow over your heart toward that person.

Not only did Christ reconcile us to God, but He has called us to be relationship restorers.

According to II Corinthians 5,
And all things are of God, who hath reconciled us to himself by Jesus Christ, and hath given to us the ministry of reconciliation;

In part, reconciliation can be done when we go to someone that we've hurt, defrauded, lied to, gossiped about, or stole from to make things right by offering an apology and making financial restitution if needed.

My husband is an associate pastor and the above Scripture takes me back to the time we met with a young married couple who were having problems. The husband stated that the wife had 'Never, not once, apologized for anything in all their years together.'

We asked the wife if that were true, and she said 'Yes' with a grin.

My husband and I looked at each other. We knew right then what the problem was. The couple had allowed the sacred space between them to become filled with *past hurts* and *unmet expectations*.

I love how Paul begins Ephesians 4:
I therefore, the prisoner of the Lord, beseech you that ye walk worthy of the vocation wherewith ye are called, with all lowliness and meekness, with longsuffering, forbearing one another in love; **endeavoring to keep the unity of the Spirit in the bond of peace.**

Four verses later, Paul writes, *Wherefore he saith, When he ascended up on high, he led captivity captive,* **and gave gifts unto men.**

In these verses, Paul is talking about Jesus. *He gave gifts.* This makes me think of the Gospel of Matthew, where Jesus says, *Therefore if thou bring thy gift to the altar, and there rememberest that thy brother hath ought against thee; Leave there thy gift before the altar, and go thy way; first be reconciled to thy brother, and then come and offer thy gift.*

Let's take a closer look at the words of Jesus. We know that everything in the New Testament can be found in the Old Testament, which includes *leaving your gift on the altar and reconciling with the person who has something against you.* We know that a good rabbi pushes the students toward the text, which is what we see here. Jesus is pushing us toward the text, but the question is, *Which text?*

Jesus is drawing our attention to the guilt offering found in the writings of Moses. There are 5 sacrificial offerings listed in the first three chapters of Leviticus,[44] which are:

1. *Olah* – burnt offering
2. *Minchah* – grain offering
3. *Zevach shelamim* – peace offering
4. *Chattat* –sin offering
5. *Asham* –guilt offering

The first three offerings mentioned above represent the offerings of Joy, Peace, and Contentment. These were not required to bring to the burnt altar of sacrifice. However, the last two offerings: *chattat* and *asham,* which is the sin offering and guilt offering, were required.

The guilt offering was offered on the altar of burnt sacrifice for unintentional sins, but it could not be offered before confession was made to the person they wronged and financial reparation was paid.

Hence, Jesus saying, "Lay your gift on the altar and go to the person..."

There was no forgiveness at the altar of sacrifice for sins willfully committed. The sacrifices made at the burnt altar of sacrifice could not take away the stain of sin. It could only cover them. It was kind of like God pulling back the landscape of the universe and sweeping their sins under it. Depending on the severity of willful sin committed, the consequence might have been banishment outside the camp, like Cain, and even death by stoning, like Achan.

We see a severe action taken against Achan who stole silver and gold and a good Babylonish garment from the spoils of Jericho. Because of his willful sin, Achan and his entire family was stoned to death outside the camp, along with his sheep and livestock. The severe punishment was to protect the community from the spread of sin in the camp.

Harsh!

Agreed! But this is how it was back then.

The *chattat* and *asham* were offerings that were brought to the altar of burnt sacrifice to restore relationship.

In Genesis 4, Abel brings of the firstlings of his flock and Cain brings of the fruit of the ground. Abel brings a sin-offering and Cain does not. One had blood and one did not. The blood sacrifice can be traced back to Adam and Eve in the garden, where blood had to be shed to cover their nakedness, and can be traced back even further, to the Lamb slain from the foundation of the world.

Cain brought fruits and vegetables, rather than a lamb or a bullock. The Scripture in Leviticus tells us that the life of the flesh is in the blood. When Cain's offering wasn't accepted because it didn't have blood, he became angry with Abel, which resulted in him killing his brother, and casting the long shadow of darkness over his own life.

I love what the LORD says next. He tells Cain, *If thou doest well, shalt thou not be accepted? And if thou doest not well, sin lieth at the door.*

Let's look closer at the words "sin lieth at the door" by reading them in the Jewish Orthodox Bible. It reads,

Chattat croucheth at the petach.[45]

There are a few things I find interesting with this. The first is that *chattat* (sin) crouches at the *petach* (door). The image of sin crouching at the door reminds me of the movie *Ghost in the Darkness,* where lions kept attacking the construction workers in Africa that were building a railroad. The word 'crouching' invokes the image of a lion crouching outside of a tent door as it waits to pounce. I Peter 5 tells us that the devil is like a roaring lion, walking about, seeking whom he may devour.

Did you catch that?

The devil waits at the tent door for us to sin.

Why?

So, he can pounce!

The second thing I find interesting is that God makes a second appeal to Cain to bring a sin-offering. The same word used for *sin* in the Hebrew is also used for *sin-offering.*[46] The words 'sin lieth at the door' can be translated "a *sin-offering croucheth at the door.*"

Whew! There is another Lion in the picture, and this One's from the tribe of Judah!

Paul says in Romans 5,
Moreover the law entered, that the offense might abound, but where sin (chattat) abounded grace did much more abound.

This is a beautiful picture of the Lion of the tribe of Judah—Jesus—defeating our adversary the devil and taking back the keys to death and the grave which were stolen in the garden.

To put it plainly, God allowed for Cain to decide which lion he wanted to pounce—grace or sin. The Scripture is clear which one Cain chose.

Which lion do you choose when you get angry?

Is it,

Separation or Reconciliation?

Is it,

Chaos or Peace?

What it really comes down to is, Who do you become when you get hurt?

Ouch!

On that note, let's circle back to II Corinthians 5, where Paul tells us,
God was hid in Christ reconciling the world unto Himself.

The invisible God wrapped Himself in human flesh, called that flesh His son, and was tented among us, so that we could be reconciled to Him through the death, burial, and resurrection process.

And like the story of Jonah, the *tent* became a backdrop of hope that all Gentiles would come into covenant with the God of two Testaments.

So, let's talk about *the gift* of reconciliation and the couple who had marital problems. I turned to the wife who had 'never, not once said she was sorry, and said to her,

"Jane, there's a Scripture that reads, If you bring your gift to the altar, and there remember that your brother has something against you, leave your gift there before the altar, and go your way. First be reconciled to your brother, and then come and offer your gift."

I looked her in the eyes, and said, "You're looking for a change in your marriage, but the change you seek only comes through reconciliation. The problem is that you are not willing to admit when you are wrong, and your unwillingness is creating distance between you. You're not willing to humble yourself and apologize when you're wrong. You want your husband to make all the concessions because you've not learned the power and the freedom of saying, 'I'm sorry.' Being quick to forgive means being quick to apologize even if you are not the initiator and even when you don't feel like it. I can tell you that Jesus was perfect, yet He took all the blame, so that humanity could be reconciled to God. It was through the gift of reconciliation that Jesus restored humanity to friendly relations."

My husband looked at her and said, "You've got to do the hard work of reconciliation, that is, if you want the walls to come down between you. Sorry shifts the atmosphere. You want peace in your marriage, then be the peacemaker."

The wife's eyes welled. She turned toward her husband and took his hands in hers. "I'm sorry," she sobbed.

There was an instant change in their relationship. The tension in the room lifted and both parties were reconciled.

God has called each one of us into the ministry of reconciliation. We can restore many relationships simply by offering grace and extending forgiveness, even when we didn't initiate the offense.

So if it be possible, put your gift on the altar and go to the person you have wronged or been wronged by and make the space between you right. Then come offer your gift to the Lord.

But the text doesn't end there! It goes on to say,
Agree with thine adversary quickly, whiles thou art in the way with him; lest at any time the adversary deliver thee to the judge, and the judge deliver thee to the officer, and thou be cast into prison.

This text refers to restitution, restoration, and reconciliation. In other words, when you wrong someone, you need to make it right, before they bring you to court. It is also a picture of what happens when you choose not to forgive—you become a prisoner by tethering yourself to the wrong done by the wrongdoer.

WHAT IF RECONCILIATION ISN'T POSSIBLE?

Reconciliation and forgiveness aren't always the same thing. Forgiveness is possible even when reconciliation is not. The definition of forgiveness is the *action or process of forgiving or being forgiven.* The river driver's main purpose was to get the logs to the mill, whether they felt like it or not. Forgiveness works the same way. Our job is to keep the *logs* flowing downstream, whether we feel like it or not.

Corrie ten Boom, the author of *The Hiding Place* recalls forgiving a prison guard at the concentration camp where she and her sister, Betsy, were held, and where Betsy would later die. The *ten Boom* family helped the Jews in Holland escape Nazi persecution by hiding them in their home. In 1944, Corrie and five family members were arrested by the German police.

One week after Betsy died in the concentration camp, Corrie was released on a clerical error. After the war ended, Corrie travelled the world preaching about forgiveness. One evening, as she was preparing to speak at a church, she looked out into the crowd and saw the prison guard who was responsible for her sister's death.

After the service, the prison guard came up to her and told her how he had become a Christian and that he wanted to hear from her that she forgave him for the inhumane acts he committed against her in the concentration camp.

Corrie felt nothing but hate as the former guard extended his hand to shake hers. She stared at his empty hand and prayed silently, "Jesus, help me! I can lift my hand. I can do that much." She told God, "You supply the feeling."

Suddenly, Corrie ten Boom looked up at the former prison guard. A warmth ran up and down her arm as she grabbed his hand and said, "I forgive you, brother! With all my heart!"[47]

Not only had she forgiven the guard, but, she had forgiven the Dutch informant that turned her family over to the German police. Even though Corrie forgave the informant, she couldn't forget the wrong, and years later, she found herself rehearsing the injustices of all that had transpired at the hands of the fellow Dutchman.

After two weeks of rehearsing the injustices and not being able to sleep at night, Corrie confided in a local pastor about what she thought was the unwillingness to forgive. The pastor pointed up at the bell in the church tower and told Corrie that the bell was rung by pulling the cord, but even after letting go of the cord, the bell would continue to swing and ring.

The pastor said to Corrie, "First a ding, then a dong, until it slows down and finally comes to a stop. I believe the same thing is true of forgiveness…when we forgive, we take our hand off the cord. But if we've been tugging at our grievances for a long time, we mustn't be surprised if the old angry thoughts keep coming for a while. They're just the ding and dongs of the old bell slowing down."

Corrie ten Boom would later tell the story of the bell, saying, "And so it proved to be. There were a few more midnight reverberations, a couple of dings when the subject came up in my conversations, but the force—which was my willingness in the matter—had gone out of them. They came less and less often and at the last stopped altogether: we can trust God not only above our emotions, but also above our thoughts."[48]

Did reconciliation take place between Corrie ten Boom and the prison guard or between Corrie ten Boom and the fellow Dutchman? No, but forgiveness did. Forgiveness is a process. Not a feeling. It begins with you putting your will in God's hands and trusting Him enough through the process. It's you taking up your pickaroon pole and each day, moving the *logs* a little further downstream, until they finally come to the place of completion, where the reverberations and even generations of bitterness and hatred stop, and God can use the logs for His glory.

Perhaps *take up your cross daily* looks a lot like a river driver with a pickaroon pole. Remember the question isn't *how* to forgive. The question is *when*. The two great equalizers are suffering and forgiveness. God wants to get the glory out of your story, but you've got to get the logs to Him first!

And just because you forgive your offender doesn't mean reconciliation is possible.

Reconciliation requires a change in relationship. This means, it may not be possible with someone you fear, someone who is unrepentant, or someone who uses shame and intimidation as control. However, forgiveness is always available even when reconciliation is not.

WHAT FORGIVENESS IS NOT

- Forgiveness is not a feeling. It is an act of the will. Jesus prayed before going to the cross, "Let this cup pass from me," but then added, "Not my will but thine be done." This is because the Spirit is willing, but the flesh is weak.
- Forgiveness does not mean sweeping it under the rug. When my parents found out what my uncle had done to me, they called the police, and he went to jail.
- Forgiveness does not mean forgetting. It's what you do with the time that heals the wounds. Forgiveness is progressive. We need to keep the logs moving forward downstream to the Mill. The moment they stop, it creates a log jam.
- Forgiveness does not mean excusing a wrong. It does not mean absence of consequence. We can forgive the person without excusing what they did.
- Forgiveness is not based on the offender's level of sorry. The offender might never admit to being sorry or even having harmed you. Whether or not the offender apologizes, we should forgive. Jesus forgave the mockers and the soldiers, and from the cross He prayed, "Father, forgive them, for they know not what they do.

Forgiveness is a must! We need to forgive no matter how big or small the wrongdoing. We need to forgive whether justice prevails or not. The highest act of love is the forgiveness we give ourselves and others.

Men at logging operation using "Steam Donkey" engine.

"Donkey Engine on Slope," accessed August 8, 2022,
https://hsuredwoodsproject.omeka.net/items/show/12, Humboldt State University Special
Collections, Boyle Collection, Identifier 1999.03.0021

7

DONKEY ENGINES & WANNIGANS

"To forgive is to set a prisoner free and discover that the prisoner was you"
— *Lewis B. Smedes*

IN THE NORTHWEST part of the United States, due to the Giant Sequoia trees and Douglas Firs, a donkey engine would be used to haul the fallen trees from the woods to the rivers or railways. A donkey engine[49] was an oversized steam engine hooked to an oversized sled and placed along a *skid road*.[50] A skid road was a dirt road overlaid with wooden slats that were slathered with animal fat and spaced apart to help glide the logs along. Skid road got its name from the many logging tents that lined the dirt road where the donkey engine was located.

Jesus calls for a donkey. You get the feeling something else is going on here, right? This donkey wasn't just any donkey. This donkey was something more. Jesus was fixing to move some logs—some fifteen hundred years' worth! It's Passover time and this scene is known in the Gospels as the Triumphal Entry.

When the Messiah approaches Jerusalem, by way of the mount of Olives, He sends two of His disciples into the village to fetch a donkey tied with her colt. He instructs them to bring the donkey and the colt back, and if any man asks them, tell them, the Lord hath need of them.

Why?

Well, because the Old Testament tells us that all this was done that the Scripture might be fulfilled,
Behold, thy king cometh unto thee, meek, and sitting upon a donkey, and a colt the foal of a donkey.

My husband was preaching recently, and said, "Have you ever noticed how all donkeys have a cross on their back?" Then he added, "They have a stripe across their shoulders and a stripe down their back. Google it."

It's true. (I Googled it.)

Which brings me back to the scripture about the donkey and the king.

In ancient Near East culture, a donkey was used for hauling material and plowing fields. It was also used as transportation. In Jewish teaching, a king riding a horse symbolized "war," while a king riding a donkey symbolized "peace." When Jesus rode in on a donkey at Passover, He was demonstrating to the Jewish audience that He was their King. Not just their King, but the King of all of mankind.

Annually, seven Feasts, otherwise called *Divine appointments* have been observed by the Jewish people for thousands of years. These appointed times are prophetic in nature.

The seven feasts[51] are as follows:

1. *Pesach* (Feast of Passover)
2. *Chag Hamotzi* (Feast of Unleavened Bread)
3. *Yom Habikkurim* (Feast of First Fruits)
4. *Shavu'ot* (Feast of Pentecost)
5. *Rosh Hashanah/Yom Teruah* (Jewish New Year or Feast of Trumpets)
6. *Yom Kippur* (Day of Atonement)
7. *Sukkot* (Feast of Tabernacles)

What is Passover?

Well, to begin with, it's a Spring feast, or as Leviticus 23 puts it, it's a 'Holy Convocation.' The word 'feast' does not mean food. The word **feast** comes from the Hebrew word *mikrah*,[52] and simply means, "rehearsal." The seven annual feasts were dress rehearsals for "something to come."

What was to come? You ask. It was the arrival of the Messiah King, of course!

As Jesus made His descent from the mount of Olives, Scripture tells us that a very great multitude spread their garments in the way; others cut down palm branches, and strewed them in the way, while others waved palm branches. The multitude went before him, and followed behind him, and cried, "Hosanna," which means, "Save now."

Save now?

Yes. Save them from their enemy—the Romans who have their boot on their necks.

And in order to understand the fifteen hundred years of Passover events leading up to Jesus' descent from the mount of Olives, you need to understand the first Passover in its context.

The very first Passover is known as the Egyptian Passover. It dates back to the Hebrew people in bondage, back to Pharaoh and the 10 plagues, back to when God told Moses to have each household apply the blood of a spotless lamb to the lintel and doorposts with a Hyssop branch, back to when the death angel saw the blood and passed over the houses, and the firstborn were spared. The death of the lamb acted as a ransom for the household. A life for a life.

Christ the Lamb of God paid the ransom for us, which is why I Peter 1 says,
Forasmuch as ye know that ye were not redeemed with corruptible things, as silver and gold, from your vain conversation received by tradition from your fathers; but with the precious blood of Christ, as of a lamb without blemish and without spot.

And why I Timothy 2 says,
Who gave himself a ransom for all, to be testified in due time.

In the book of Exodus, the Lord tells Moses to have the Jewish people observe Passover each year, year after year, continually. Each year, every household was expected to kill a Passover lamb on the evening of Passover and eat it with bitter herbs and unleavened bread.

It is told in Jewish literature that during the wilderness wanderings the Jewish people observed Passover in the first year of freedom, and that for the next 39 years they did not, because as Rabbi Shmuel Kogan writes in an article on Passover, "During the forty years we traveled through the desert, although the holiday was presumably observed, the only time we brought the Paschal Offering [Passover Lamb] was on the Exodus' first anniversary. The next time the

Jewish people brought this offering was 39 years later, when they entered Israel."[53]

Hmmm...interesting! How many stripes did Jesus take?

39

Just a thought. Maybe, just maybe, Jesus as the substitutionary sacrifice for our sins, took one stripe for each year the Jewish people failed to sacrificially offer one Passover lamb per household in observance of the annual holiday during the wilderness wanderings as the LORD commanded Moses.

According to the Jewish Encyclopedia and The Temple Institute, the priests gave each Passover lamb a drink from a silver cup before slitting its throat. After slitting its throat, the priests would catch the blood in a silver vessel with a rounded bottom to be sprinkled on the altar.

But wait!—that's not the best part—on the *Feast of Passover*, which is the day Christ died, Jesus, the spotless Lamb of God said these two words while nailed to the cross, "I thirst." After which He was given a drink *just* before He died.

Did you catch that? The feasts are prophetic in nature. Here, Jesus fulfilled even the smallest of details.

Just think of the images invoked by Jesus descending the mount of Olives on the back of a donkey during the parade of lambs. Jesus is the new Moses and there is a second exodus on the horizon.

The first Exodus was about God's chosen people being rescued from bondage.

The second Exodus was about all people being rescued from the bondage of sin and death.

What happened on the Egyptian Passover was not just for the Jewish people in captivity, and not just for the making of a good movie starring Charleston Heston, but for us, here and now.

The first Exodus brought...

Deliverance,

Redemption,

And freedom from Pharaoh to a particular people group.

The Second Exodus brought...

Deliverance,

Redemption,

and the forgiveness of sins to all people groups.

Hasn't Passover always been about the forgiveness of sins? you ask.

No. Never. Not once.

In the fifteen hundred years prior to the death of Jesus, the yearly Passover celebration never included the forgiveness of sins. Basically, what the Jewish people had was the 'rolling ahead of sins' or as Rabbi Mordecai Griffin said, "Kicking the can down the road."[54] The daily sacrifices, the weekly sacrifice, the monthly sacrifice, and the sacrifices offered during the seven special feasts couldn't take away their sins. It just kicked them down the road a bit.

There was no remission of sins. There was only the covering of sins. For fifteen hundred years, on the Day of Atonement, God pulled back the landscape of the universe and swept *their* sins under it, at least that is, until Christ showed up.

In N.T. Wright's article, Tracing Atonement Through the Story of Scripture, he writes,

> *"The Passover event, with its liberation from Egyptian slavery, signaled God was King (Exodus 15:18). God had not abandoned his people. The Exodus event doesn't mention atonement, but it becomes important to how the New Testament writers understood the death of Jesus."[55]*

Five paragraphs later, Wright quotes a passage from his book, *The Day the Revolution Began:*

> *"When Jesus wanted to explain to his followers what his forthcoming death was all about, he did not give them a theory, a model, a metaphor, or any other such thing; he gave them a meal."[56]*

Wright goes on to say,

> *"Jesus transformed the Passover meal from looking back towards the Exodus to looking forward to his pending death. The cup of wine was the blood of the covenant which is poured out for many for the forgiveness of sins (Matthew 26:28 ESV)."[57]*

At the Last Supper, Jesus makes the Passover meal about Himself.

He wants the disciples to know that…
He is all in all.

He wants them to know that...

He is...

The Lamb of God.

He is...

The Door of Salvation.

He is...

The High Priest.

He is...

the Offerer and the Offering.

The One who offers the sacrifice becomes the Sacrifice.

Luke's account of the Triumphal Entry takes us down *skid road*. It starts off with a blind man whom Jesus heals near Jericho and is followed by the story of Zacchaeus, a sinful tax collector. As Jesus makes His way toward Jerusalem, He notices Zacchaeus in the Sycamore tree and calls him down to tell him that He was going home with him today.

I love this—Jesus was controversial. Always doing the jaw-dropping next best thing. He didn't come to do away with the law; He came to perfect it and to fulfill it by providing new interpretations and by opening their understandings to new ideas. This is why *Jesus spent so much time on skid road with...*
publicans and sinners,
the poor,
the oppressed,

the downtrodden,
the underdog,
the marginalized,
the outcast,
the unclean.
And why He spent so little time with the religious leaders of the day.

Did you know that the Passover lambs were chosen from a flock in Bethlehem?

I know what you're thinking. *What's all this got to do with river drivers and logs?*

The answer is—
Everything!

We know that John the Baptist calls Jesus the Lamb of God and that the Lamb of God was born in Bethlehem. An estimated 250,000 lambs at Passover were paraded down the streets of Jerusalem while the Jewish people shouted, "Blessed is he who comes in the name of the LORD" and waived palm branches in celebration as the lambs passed. The Passover lambs were taken from the flock in Bethlehem.

Hmm.

It is during this parade, that Jesus calls for a donkey in fulfillment of the yearly "dress rehearsal."

What does this mean exactly?

It means that no matter how many special sacrifices and services the high priest and Levites performed each year, they never got it right. The blood of bulls and of goats could not take away the sins of the people. Day after day, month after month, year after year, for fifteen hundred years, the feasts were *just* that—'dress rehearsals'—in preparation for *something to come*, which we know is Jesus, who is the ultimate Sacrifice for our sins, who through the cross reconciled all things to God. The love of God is far reaching. It reaches all the way back before sin entered the world to the Lamb slain from the foundation of the world, and is forward moving, for all those not yet born.

And get this! The 'dress rehearsal' for the feast of Passover was fulfilled by Jesus on the feast of Passover (or Feast of Freedom). Jesus was both the Great High Priest and the Lamb slain from the foundation of the world. Upon His death, burial, and resurrection, the Jewish sacrificial system became ineffective. The need to rehearse was no longer needed, for that which was *to come* had finally *come*. Through the death of the Lamb of God, who's blood was applied to the universal doorpost as a ransom once and for all, for all, we are rescued. His life for ours.

Now let's look at Bethlehem and its meaning in the Hebrew language. It means, "The House of Bread." To break it down further, *bet* means, house, and *lachem* or *lekhem* means, bread.[58]

Not only does John call Jesus,

The Door

and

The Lamb of God,

but he also calls Him,

The Bread of Life.

Ray Vander Laan puts it this way: "The Bread of Life was born in a bakery."[59]

But wait! There's more! As stated before, every Hebrew word has numeric value. There are 22 letters in the Hebrew alphabet. Each letter has a word picture and a numerical value to convey deeper insights and meanings. In Hebrew the numerical value of *Bethlehem* or *House of Bread* is 490. The sum of 490 in the Hebrew language means "**complete**" or "**perfect**" or "**finished**."[60]

We know that Jesus died so that we could have forgiveness of sins and that forgiveness is connected to daily *bread* in the Lord's Prayer:
Give us this day our daily bread. And forgive us our debts, as we forgive our debtors.

In Matthew 18, Peter asks,
Lord, how many times shall my brother sin against me and I still forgive him? Up to seven times?[61]

Well, that's a logical assumption seems how the number seven means "completeness" in Hebrew. But look at what Jesus tells Peter. He says, *Forgive seventy times seven.*

I know what you're thinking, it's easier to forgive than do the math, but Jesus' response wasn't *just* about forgiving endlessly or unconditionally. It was also about the sum of the numbers—seventy times seven is 490.

Other than Jesus telling Peter to forgive 490 times, where else have we seen this number?

Right. It's the Hebraic value of Bethlehem or *House of Bread.*

And what is the meaning of 490 again?

Complete.

Perfect.

Finished.

But wait! That's not all!

According to Rabbi Jason Sobel the number 490 is also the value of the Hebrew text "Let your heart be perfect."

Which leaves me to wonder,
What happens when we don't forgive?

In Matthew 18, immediately following Jesus telling Peter to forgive 70x7, He shares this parable:

> *Therefore, the kingdom of heaven is like a king who wanted to settle accounts with his servants. As he began the settlement, a man who owed him ten thousand bags of gold was brought to him. Since he was not able to pay, the master ordered that he and his wife and his children and all that he had be sold to repay the debt.*
>
> *At this the servant fell on his knees before him. 'Be patient with me,' he begged, 'and I will pay back everything.' The servant's master took pity on him, canceled the debt and let him go.*
>
> *But when that servant went out, he found one of his fellow servants who owed him a hundred silver coins. He grabbed him and began to choke him. 'Pay back what you owe me!' he demanded.*
>
> *His fellow servant fell to his knees and begged him, 'Be patient with me, and I will pay it back.'*
>
> *But he refused. Instead, he went off and had the man thrown into prison until he could pay the debt. When the*

other servants saw what had happened, they were outraged and went and told their master everything that had happened.

Then the master called the servant in. 'You wicked servant,' he said, 'I canceled all that debt of yours because you begged me to. Shouldn't you have had mercy on your fellow servant just as I had on you?' In anger his master handed him over to the jailers to be tortured, until he should pay back all he owed. This is how my heavenly Father will treat each of you unless you forgive your brother or sister from your heart.[62]

According to Jesus the answer is clear, if you choose not to forgive, you will be handed over to the jailer to be tortured.

Seriously?!

Yes, there are spiritual, physical, and mental repercussions that involve various forms of anguish. When R.T. Kendall began to study forgiveness in the 80's, he was shocked to find that up until the last two decades the doctrine of forgiveness been greatly overlooked by the church. He writes in his book *Total Forgiveness*:

"Social scientists are discovering that forgiveness may help lead to victim's emotional and even physical healing and wholeness. As recently as the early 1980s, Dr. Glen Hamden went to the University of Kansas library and looked up the word forgiveness in Psychological Abstracts. He couldn't find a single reference. But things are changing. Former President Jimmy Carter, Archbishop Desmond Tutu, and former missionary Elisabeth Elliot have been promoting a $10 million "Campaign for Forgiveness Research," established as a nonprofit corporation to attract donations that will support forgiveness research proposals. In 1998 the John Templeton Foundation awarded research

grants for the study of forgiveness to twenty-nine scholars, and one of the primary discoveries of these studies is that the person who gains the most from forgiveness is the person who does the forgiving."[63]

When you pray this prayer, "Give us this day our daily bread. And forgive us our debts, as we forgive our debtors," you are asking God to forgive you of your sins. The word 'debt' or 'trespasses' can both be used to mean *sins*.

In the parable about the servant's debt:

1. The king had empathy on the servant
2. The king cancelled the servant's debt/forgave the trespasses
3. The king let the servant go

Just like a river driver, the king in the parable used the peavey hook to turn the *logs* over and see the situation through the *lens of empathy*. By putting the servant's sandals on, he was able to extend compassion and mercy.

The peavey hook is an essential tool in keeping our hearts pure. Not all offenses are intentional, and by using the peavey hook it helps us to see why the person may have said what they said or did what they did. *Things aren't always what they seem.*

Rabbi Mordecai Griffin tells a story about a Rabbi friend of his. Before each counseling session, his friend would change into the clothes of the people he was about to counsel. Rabbi Griffin said this about the friend; "He came down on their level, in order to raise them up."[64] This isn't the first time in history that's been done. In the New Testament, God clothed Himself in human flesh and was tented among us. The invisible God made Himself visible. When we couldn't get to Him, He came down on our level to raise us up. For that reason alone, it makes sense to me, that if God saw fit to use the peavey hook to reconcile us to Himself, then we should be willing to use the peavey hook to be reconciled one to another. Scripture tells us that we have been given the ministry of reconciliation. *Which means there's no excuses!*

Some time ago, I was watching Super Soul Sunday. Brené Brown, who is a shame researcher asked Oprah this question, "What is a story that has one or two limited data points and we fill the rest in with fear?" Before Oprah could answer, Brené responded with "A conspiracy theory."[65]

Brené proceeded to say, "A confabulation is a lie told honestly. When something hard happens, our emotions get the first crack of making sense of things. We think we're rational beings and that cognition is going to make sense of it and carry us through. Emotion is driving, while thought and behavior are in the trunk."[66]

We do this all the time, don't we?

We take one or two limited pieces of data and fill in the blanks with fear. The devil is the accuser of the brethren and will do whatever he can. This includes causing division through misunderstandings to get us off track and keep us there. The peavey hook helps us turn offenses over and look at them a different way. This keeps the logs from stacking up in our lives and creating log jams. The truth is that the devil doesn't want us to be happy. He surely doesn't want us to have a healthy quality of life in the present, which is where abundant life starts, here, now.

RELEASE THEM AND SET THEM FREE

Until we release the offender and set them free, we carry the trauma associated with the tragedy in our body and in our nervous system. Every time we see our offender, hear a certain sound, smell a certain smell, and sometimes even taste a certain taste, it triggers the pain of the past. This causes the past to become present with us.

Bitterness, resentment, hard feelings, and dark emotions can cause deep mental anguish, making us act and react irrationally. Trauma steps out of time, and until we heal from the trauma, time can't start back up. Which means, the past is never the past, the past is always present, allowing trauma to run roughshod in our lives.

When my boys were young, we had a baby turtle named Rondo that lived in a fish tank with water, rocks, and a plastic log house. Every day, we would take Rondo out of the tank to play with him and put him back in the tank when we were done. Shortly after purchasing Rondo, we started feeling bad about keeping him trapped in the tank, alone without a turtle friend to keep him company. We wanted to let him go, but we didn't want him to die, so we kept him.

One day, we were listening to the Dan Le Batard show, and a zoologist came on who was fielding questions, and a caller asked, "Can you release a pet turtle into the wild without it dying?" The zoologist said, "Yes. A turtle will adapt. They won't die." Well, that's all my husband and I needed to hear. That day, we took Rondo to the pond by the library and **set him free**. I'll never forget watching Rondo slide down the embankment into the water. He was a natural swimmer. He paddled out a few feet, nipped at a goldfish going by, and then kept swimming.

Up until that point, we were good at playing "catch and release."

We do this with our offenders, catch and release, that is. We release the offender in the spirit of forgiveness, and then, when the notion fades, we catch them, and put them back in the prison or the log boom that is our mind. Until the next time the spirit of forgiveness hits us, and we release them again, only to catch them again. Forgiveness is counterintuitive. It goes against logic and reason.

I know what you are thinking. *Forgive them so I can be free? That doesn't make any sense!*

I know! That's what I've been trying to tell you.

Forgiveness starts with a decision, yes, but it doesn't end there. It ends at the Mill, where God repurposes the pain and the suffering on purpose for a purpose. It's where the trauma becomes the treasure.

As a River Jack and a River Jill, we must do the hard work of getting our logs to the Mill. First, we release the offender and set them free in our heart and mind. Second, we do the hard work of steering the logs downstream, until they reach the place of Completion.

That means, no more catch and release, or better said, no more mental log booms. Freeing the logs from a mental boom doesn't get the logs to the Mill. We do! And we do this with the pickaroon pole and the peavey hook. We must keep turning them over and steering them downstream. Forgiveness is a process, and that process begins with awareness.

But they're not sorry!

They never apologized, you say.

It doesn't matter!

Forgiveness is a daily process and is forward moving. It's only natural to experience reverberations from the old bell as it slows down before it comes to a complete stop. The devil will try to make this reverberation feel like a setback. Don't let him!

Dr. Phil said, "Whoever said, 'Time heals all wounds lied.' It's what you do with the time that heals the wounds." In other words, keep your pickaroon poles out in front, and keep those logs moving downstream toward the Mill.

IF YOU WANT TO BE FORGIVEN, YOU MUST FORGIVE OTHERS

The same servant who was forgiven of a large debt, refused to forgive his fellow servant of a small debt. He demanded payment and when his fellow servant couldn't pay, he choked him and threw him in jail. The people who saw this became angry and took the matter to the king. When the king found out, he turned the wicked servant over to the jailer to be tortured until he could repay the debt.

Consider these words of Jesus in Matthew 5,

> *Therefore, if you are offering your gift at the altar and there remember that your brother or sister has something against you, leave your gift there in front of the altar. First go and be reconciled to them; then come and offer your gift.*
>
> *Settle matters quickly with your adversary who is taking you to court. Do it while you are still together on the way, or your adversary may hand you over to the judge, and the judge may hand you over to the officer, and you may be thrown into prison. Truly I tell you, you will not get out until you have paid the last penny.*[67]

The king in Matthew 18 and the judge in Matthew 5 are the same person. In ancient Near East culture, the king's duties included judging the people. If a person had something against their brother, and the one who did the wrong failed to make it right, then the matter would be brought before the king to be judged.

Now compare that with the words of Jesus in Matthew 7,
*Judge not, that ye be not judged. For with what judgment ye judge, ye shall be judged: and with what measure ye mete, **it shall be measured to you** again.*

You quickly realize that Jesus was talking about forgiveness. For with what measure you forgive; you will be forgiven. The wicked servant didn't forgive his fellow servant, and in return, he was given over to the tormentor. *I bet he wished he forgave!*

Have you ever wondered why forgiveness isn't mentioned as one of the fruits of the Spirit in Galatians 5?

Here's the list:
Love.
Joy.
Peace.
Longsuffering.
Gentleness.
Goodness.
Faith.
Meekness.
Temperance.

That's because forgiveness isn't a fruit. It's the tree! The fruit of the Spirit hang on the branches of forgiveness. Without forgiveness there can be no fruit. The evidence of forgiveness is the presence of fruit. If you forgive abundantly, you will have fruit abundantly. If you forgive little, you will have little fruit in your life. For what measure you give; it will come back to you. A lack of love, joy, and peace would indicate a lack of forgiveness.

In Luke 10, a certain lawyer asks Jesus, "Who is my neighbor?"

To a Jewish audience, the phrase "my neighbor" largely implied *anyone Jewish.* Which was why Jesus tells the parable of the Good Samaritan. He was opening their eyes to the Divine by giving them a new interpretation, a new narrative, a new expectation to the second greatest commandment, which is to "love thy neighbor as thyself." The first, and greatest commandment is to "Love the Lord thy God with all thy heart, and with all thy soul, and with all thy mind." Jesus says the second commandment is like the first. In other words, when you love people, you love God. The Bible isn't just a guide on how to get to heaven, but it is a guide on how to bring heaven down to us. God is love. And that love includes all people. To love thy neighbor isn't just for the Jewish people way back then, or for the Jewish people now, but it's for all people everywhere. To love means to forgive. You can't have one without the other.

You mean, I must love...

My worst enemy?
Yes!

My impatient boss?
Yes!

The tenant who stiffed me?
Yes!

The person who returned my lawn mower broken?
Yes!

The teacher who said I would never amount to anything?
Yes!

My mother who gave me up for adoption?
Yes!

My alcoholic father?
Yes!

The offender who hurt my child?
Yes!

Love is forgiveness in disguise. It's the big, loopy stitches by which the whole gospel is held together. For God so loved that He gave. Look at these words of Jesus in Luke 6,

> *If you love those who love you, what credit is that to you? Even sinners love those who love them. And if you do good to those who are good to you, what credit is that to you? Even sinners do that. And if you lend to those from whom you expect repayment, what credit is that to you? Even sinners lend to sinners, expecting to be repaid in full. But love your enemies, do good to them, and lend to them without expecting to get anything back. Then your reward will be great, and you will be children of the Most High, because he is kind to the ungrateful and wicked. Be merciful, just as your Father is merciful.*[68]

Or these words of Paul in Colossians 3,
Bear with each other and forgive one another if any of you has a grievance against someone. Forgive as the Lord forgave you.[69]

Or these words in Ephesians 4,
Be kind to one another, tenderhearted, forgiving one another, as God in Christ forgave you.[70]

I love that part—
Be kind.

UNFORGIVENESS WILL COST YOU

Many years ago, I was watching the Montel Williams Show. There was a guest on that owed the IRS three dollars. The guest didn't know he owed the IRS money, until years later, when he received a bill in the mail. What started as a three-dollar debt ended up costing him thousands in interest.

What I'm saying is,
Unforgiveness accrues daily. What begins as insignificant will cost
you more then you expect in the end.

Which makes me think of the Hebrew Scripture,
It's the little foxes that spoil the vine.

Listen! God wants all your logs—even the small ones! If you have
any bitterness or anger or resentment toward anyone, in any area,
then it's time to forgive: *For if ye forgive men their trespasses, your
heavenly Father will also forgive you.*

The same chapter in Matthew where Jesus says,
*Therefore, if you are offering your gift at the altar and there
remember that your brother or sister has something against
you, leave your gift there in front of the altar. First go and be
reconciled to them...*[71]

ends with Jesus saying,
*Be ye therefore perfect, even as your Father which is in heaven is
perfect.*

Was Jesus really telling them to be *perfect* as their Father which is
in heaven is perfect? Or was he telling them to forgive, and in
forgiving one another's trespasses their hearts would be free of
obstacles and debris? Thus, fulfilling the meaning of the Hebraic
value 70x7= **Perfect**.

It's through the process of forgiving one another that we fulfill the
Hebrew text, *Let your heart be perfect* and personify the meaning of
490.

EVERY RIVER DRIVER NEEDS A WANNIGAN
What's a wannigan? you ask.
Well, it's the floating cook shack, of course!

The wannigan provided the river drivers with food and supplies on the river and followed them downstream as they worked[72]. The river drivers worked from sunup to sundown clearing log jams and steering logs in a forward motion down river. They relied heavily on the cooks aboard the cook shack to keep them hydrated and nourished. The river drivers ate breakfasts at 4 A.M., their first lunch at 9 A.M., a second lunch in the afternoon, and then supper. Their meals were high in carbs and proteins to help maintain their energy: canned beef, boiled ham, boiled eggs, biscuits, donuts, cookies, baked beans, and flapjacks.

Having grown up in Maine, flapjacks were a staple. A flapjack is a very large, very dense pancake, that serves as a reminder of the hard-working river drivers and lumberjacks of that era who ate them. To the Jewish people, bread served as a daily reminder of God's provisions in the wilderness. They ate white wafers that fell from heaven, kept a golden pot of manna in the Ark of the Covenant, celebrated Passover with seven days of unleavened bread, and maintained twelve loaves of bread in the Holy Place. The twelve loaves are also known as the *Bread of Presence.*

When Jesus proclaimed that he was *the Bread of Life which came down from heaven,* the religious leaders of that day picked up stones to cast at Him. They understood His claim to Deity. And when Jesus broke bread with His disciples, telling them to, *Take, eat this is my body which is broken for you. This do in remembrance of me,* He transformed the Passover meal from looking backward to looking forward. When Jesus connected daily bread to forgiveness, He was showing them the importance of *His Presence* in their lives. For them to experience *His Presence* in a consistent way, they needed to keep their hearts pure through the daily process of forgiveness.

The same is true for us—If we want *His Presence* without restriction in our lives, we need to keep our hearts free of obstacles and debris. In order to do that, we need to pick up the pickaroon pole and be willing to, each day, steer the *logs of offense* forward until they come to the place of Completion, where God can use them, and where the payment of 'double for your shame' is paid out.

It's no wonder the Apostle Paul writes so frequently about reconciliation in his letters to the churches. We must be watchful and work hard and fast to prevent log jams. It's through the renewed process of turning logs over and steering them downstream that we apply the words of our Savior to our daily lives. That is, to be perfect as our Father which is in Heaven is perfect.

River Driver moving logs down the river.

Photo credit and permission to use by David Calder

8

THE SCAPEGOAT & THE RIVER DRIVER

"We are not forgiven because we are good. We are forgiven because Christ bore our sins"

— Joseph Prince

FEAST NUMBER SIX on the Jewish calendar is known as *Yom Kippur* or the Day of Atonement. It is the most important holiday on the Jewish calendar. The Day of Atonement is where we get the word 'scapegoat' from and it is the only day the high priest can enter behind the veil into the Holy of Holies. The Hebrew word for Scapegoat is *Azazel*,[73] which means, to take away. In today's world, we refer to a *scapegoat* as a person who takes the blame or fall for someone else.

What does the scapegoat have to do with forgiveness? you ask.

That's a good question. The answer is simple.
Everything!

Forgiveness is Divine, which means, it is a God idea!

To the Jewish people, forgiveness is a temporary state and therefore needs annual renewal. For fifteen hundred years up to the destruction of the second temple in 70 AD, the high priest would take two identical and spotless goats on the Day of Atonement and cast lots over them. Then, depending on how the lots fell, the goat designated 'For the LORD' would have its throat cut and its blood sprinkled on the Mercy Seat as a special sacrifice, while the other goat would be designated the scapegoat. This was a Jewish tradition, where the high priests would place a scarlet cord around the scapegoat's head, lay his hands on its head, and then symbolically transfer the sins of Israel to it. After the sin transfer was complete, the scapegoat would then be led several miles into the wilderness by the red cord, symbolically carrying away the sins of Israel for another year.

According to the Mishnah, which is a Jewish commentary dating back thousands of years, the one appointed with the task of leading the scapegoat away would remove the scarlet cord from the scapegoat's head, before leaving the goat in the wilderness. There is endless speculation about the scapegoat. Some resources indicate that it would be pushed off a cliff by the one leading it away to ensure the scapegoat loaded down with the sins of Israel did not appear in the camp the next day. The Mishnah records that the scarlet cord retrieved from the scapegoat would be hung on the temple door or the altar area and that at some point throughout the year it would miraculously turn white. *Amazing—huh?!*

But nowhere in Scripture does it mention the scarlet cord on the scapegoat's head, unless of course you're reading Isaiah, which says, "Though your sins be as scarlet, they shall be white as snow."

One morning, as I was getting ready for work, I was thinking about the scapegoat carrying away the sins of the Jewish people on the Day of Atonement and Jesus' words on the cross—*It is finished.* Suddenly, the image of the scapegoat and the image of Jesus on the cross made me think of a Maine log drive, where the *river drivers* pushed logs downstream with their pickaroon poles and peavey hooks, singing, shouting, and carrying on as they moved the logs up to a 100 miles away. As I thought about the centuries of scapegoating, the innocent God-Man on the cross, and a bunch of river drivers pushing logs downstream to the mill, a thought about forgiveness popped in my head: *Maybe what we should be saying isn't how do I forgive, but* **when...**

In that moment, I realized three things:

1. There is a process to forgiveness. No two processes are alike.
2. There is a place of Completion.
3. There is a distinction between the process and the place of Completion. They are not the same.

The **when** versus the **how** got me thinking about the phrase "Let them off the hook" and how these words can be confusing and frustrating to someone grappling with the emotional pain associated with the offense. Yes, forgiveness starts with a decision, but it doesn't end there. Depending on how deeply rooted the emotional pain is and how great the injustice is, the process to forgive can vary. How do you tell the person to let the parent who abandoned them, the spouse who cheated on them, the family member who hurt them, the thief who robbed them, the liar who lied on them, the murderer, the child abuser, the rapist, the bigot, the judgmental saint, or the calloused leader off the hook? *What does that even mean?*

(Seriously though! The words make me picture a meat hook in a butcher shop)

Yes, forgiveness is necessary. No, it is not a one-and-done. Whether we realize it or not, there is a process that leads up to the place of Completion, just like the fifteen hundred years of rolling the sins of

Israel ahead and the river drivers steering 30,000 tons of wood downstream to the mill a hundred miles away.

Although I get what is meant by the words 'Let them off the hook,' it fails to prepare the forgiver for the reverberations of the old bell as it slows down before it finally comes to a stop. The reverberations being the bitterness, the anger, the resentment, the emotional pain that one may experience the next day—the next month—the next year—even after saying, "I forgive you" for all the world to hear. It fails to prepare the *forgiver* for the necessary process of taking up their pickaroon pole daily and steering the *logs* downstream to the Mill, to the place that is Complete, Perfect, and Finished. To the place where 70x7 is 490. To the place where God will take the *raw timbers of offense* and turn them into a finished product. To the place where the glory of God is revealed in you and through you, because you finished the log drive, because your logs were converted. To the place where you remember differently, and the trauma transitions into growth for yourself and wisdom for others.

The Hebrew word for forgive is *Nasa*,[74] which means, "to carry, to lift up, to take away, to bear."

Sound familiar?
Azazel.
Scapegoat.
To take away.

In all of Israel's doings, in all their dress rehearsals, in all the Days of Atonement dating all the way back to the very first one at Mount Sinai, where Moses broke the tablets of stone in anger, their sins were never truly gone. Because in these sacrifices there is a reminder of sin.

Take this verse from Hebrews 10,

For it is not impossible for the blood of bulls and goats to take away sins.

And this,

For since the law has but a shadow of the good things to come instead of the true form of these realities, it can never, by the same sacrifices that are continually offered every year, make perfect those who draw near.[75]

The cross is the hinge on which the Old Covenant and the New Covenant hang. The dress rehearsals and sacrificial symbols all pointed forward to Calvary, even before the foundation of the world was laid, the Lamb was slain for our sins in the mind of God.

The prophet Isaiah wrote,
*Surely, he hath borne our griefs and **carried** our sorrows; yet we esteemed him stricken, smitten of God, and afflicted.*

- The scapegoat had to be without blemish…
  Pilate said, "I find no fault in Him."

- The high priest placed a scarlet cord on the scapegoat's head…
  The soldier placed a crown of thorns on Jesus' head that produced a red ring like the cord on the scapegoat's head.

- The scapegoat was taken away…
  Jesus was led away by the soldiers as the crowd shouted, "Take him away."

Why do the writers of the Gospels include such details?

Because the writers wanted us to make the connection between the scapegoat in the Old Testament and the universal Scapegoat in the New Testament. And let's not forget, on the Day of Atonement there were two identical goats—one was loaded down with the sins of the people and led away into the wilderness, while the other was a special sacrifice 'For the LORD' for the sins of Israel that occurred during the calendar year.

This is a picture of how the work of salvation overlaps in many ways. Because Jesus was all God and all man, He could fulfill the roles of the special sacrifice, the scapegoat, and the High Priest, simultaneously.

The blood from the special sacrifice was applied to the Mercy Seat, and the high priest would appear from behind the veil and stand in the tent door to announce to the Jewish audience, "*tam v'nishlam.*"[76] In Hebrew this means, "It is finished." Though we know that under the sacrificial system it was never *finished*, for what the blood of bulls and goats could not do, Jesus accomplished on the cross. With 39 brush strokes, God created the ultimate masterpiece. Calvary is God's message of forgiveness to humanity painted on a human canvas.

The same words the high priest used on the Day of Atonement; Jesus used on the cross. The Jewish bystanders would have taken *tetelestai,* which is the Greek equivalent of "tam v'nishlam" to mean, "It is finished."

As our Great High Priest, Christ made final atonement, fulfilling the work of salvation through His own death, burial, and resurrection, and was the personification of 490: **complete, perfect, finished**. Therefore, bringing an end to the temple administration and animal sacrifices required under the Old Covenant.

Here's something else that's amazing…

According to Rabbi Jack Moline, the Hebrew word for "It is finished" is used when a Jewish author completes the writing of a sacred book. The Jewish author does not use the words "the end." Instead, they will use "tam v'nishlam," which is to signify to the reader that the purpose of the work has been achieved in its fullness."

The New Testament is the New Covenant and according to the book of Hebrews, the New Covenant could not go in force until the Testator died.

Fullness.

Complete.

Finished.

Perfect.

Maybe, just maybe, the New Covenant doesn't begin with the book of Matthew as we suppose. Maybe, just maybe, it begins with the book of Acts.

It makes perfect sense how Jesus the Author and Finisher of our faith would end such a sacred book as the Old Testament with the words "It is finished." *Tam v'nishlam* to signify the purpose of the work had been accomplished in its fullness, while at the same time, the Greek equivalent *tetelestai* to signify our sin debt had been paid in full.

The good news is that what happened on the cross was not just for the Jewish people, but for the entire human race. All sin-debt past, present, and future has been forgiven—paid in full—atoned for—remitted—carried away—blotted out.

Remember the place of Completion didn't happen overnight, it happened over fifteen hundred years of dress rehearsals and spanned more than twenty-five-hundred years of man's history, dating from Moses back to Adam.

That's four-thousand years!

And since everything natural has a spiritual parallel, the logs of offense that we carry in our bodies and in our minds have a place of completion, too. A place that if we keep the pickaroon pole out in front and the bitterness, the resentment, the negative emotions, experiences, and traumatic events moving forward until they reach the Mill, we gain the skill and ability to help other river drivers maneuver their *logs* downstream to the place of Completion.

Like Paul wrote, The Good News is that *God was in Christ, reconciling the world to Himself.*

And not only that, but He has made us ministers of reconciliation. Thus, making forgiveness not only Divine, but essential to Christian living.

Who knows what masterpiece God will make with your logs—a book, a song, a movement—I can't do the doing for you, you have to do that, but I can think of at least **490** reasons why you should keep pushing, keep steering, keep moving your logs downstream.

Early logging camp

Photo credit: West Branch Historical Preservation Committee,
http://themaineboomhouses.org/photos-from-the-past/

9

THE LOGGING CAMP & THE CANT HOOK

"Grief is the root of all unforgiveness" – Brené Brown

AFTER A LOSS, grief is like a string that wraps around your finger and causes you to *remember, not to forget* the pain and the anguish of a single traumatic event. It makes you feel guilty and hampers you down with regret, what ifs, and blame—lots of it! You regret not being a better daughter or son; a better parent. You regret not kissing them goodbye. You regret the argument. You regret not telling them how beautiful, amazing, and intelligent they were. You regret not listening to your gut. Then you wonder, Did they know that I loved them? Did they call out for me? Did they suffer? And then you think, what if I would have told them not to go? What if I wouldn't have eaten *that* can of Spaghetti O's?

I know what you're thinking. *Did she just say, "Spaghetti O's?"*

Yes. Yes, I did. Let me explain.

I was fifteen years old, and it had been six weeks since I last saw my immediate family. All but Charlene, my twin sister, that is. After years of being in the Naval reserves, my dad re-enlisted in the Navy and completed boot camp for a second time. After which, he received his orders to move to Alameda, California for one year, and then from there, he would be stationed in Norfolk, Virginia.

Charlene and I didn't want to move to California. We didn't want to leave our church, our friends, our youth group, or our Bible Quiz team for a one-year stint in California, just to be uprooted again to Virginia. Our parents agreed to let us stay in Maine with our aunt, uncle, and their five children, who attended the same church as us.

It was noontime and my aunt and I were playing Chinese Checkers by the window, when the pastor's teenage son pulled into the driveway to pick up Richard, my favorite cousin and best friend. He was seventeen at the time and had just gotten his driver's license. Richard grabbed his duffle bag, kissed his mom on the cheek, and smiled at all of us.

"See you in a week," Richard said, making his infamous "whoop...whoop...whoop" sound as one of the Three Stooges before exiting.

The words, *Don't go!—stay!* ran through my head, but it was too late. He was gone. I returned my attention to the board game, and for my next move, jumped over four red marbles to the other side for the win.

Cheers erupted.

Two days later, I got up early to go babysit in the next town over. Come lunch time, I was hungry, and as I heated up a can of Beanie Weenie's for the kids, I spotted a can of Spaghetti O's in the cabinet with mini meatballs in it—*my favorite!* But remembering it was my fast day, and being a dedicated Bible Quizzer, I put the can back.

An hour later, my stomach was grumbling loudly, and I returned to the kitchen, held the can opener in my hand and eyeballed the legless *Spaghetti O* man.

Just as my stomach was about to win, Richard's face popped in my head. *It was strange.* I could sense something was wrong, and suddenly, I knew I was supposed to fast for him, intercede on his behalf, and so I put the can back.

An hour later, I returned to the cabinet. *Nothing's wrong with Richard! Stop being silly,* I told myself as I opened the can of Spaghetti O's.

Six hours later, Richard was dead!

Richard was staying at the pastor's camp and had taken the tractor down to the lake to go fishing, while the pastor's son stayed behind for a nap. When my cousin didn't return by dark, the pastor's son went looking for him and found him dead, crushed between a boulder and the tractor.

Charlene and I didn't find out until 2 o'clock in the morning when the phone rang, and the voice on the other end said, "Richard's dead!"

Tears erupted.

We knew something was wrong *even* before that because the phone rang at midnight, and we heard Richard's name, followed by a blood curdling scream. We watched as his family sprinted to the car, leaving us there alone. We waited by the phone for it to ring, crying and pleading with God the whole time.

I prayed for Richard to be injured, maimed, even paralyzed, but not dead! Dead wasn't a choice. Anything but dead. *Please God!*

When the news came by way of the phone, the shock sent me to my knees; no words would come, only guttural sounds. I wished to take his place. I wished to be dead. *I wished I didn't eat that can of Spaghetti O's!*

Suddenly, my cousin's beautiful family and the big white farmhouse filled with love, laughter, Three Stooges impressions, Chinese Checkers, church friends, and God, now seemed void of it all. And over the next year, while living in Richard's house, attending high school without him, going to Sunday School without him, taking walks without him, and looking into the empty eyes of his family, I remembered how I should have heeded God's warning—*I killed Richard!* The secret that *he appeared to me,* and I sold him for a can of Spaghetti O's gnawed at me, deepening my grief and sorrow. *I was supposed to intervene! God chose me!*

It all sounds so silly now as I type this out, but at the time, the guilt and the shame were all very real. For years, I kept the secret locked away, and at times even today, I still catch myself wondering, *What if I wouldn't have eaten that can of Spaghetti O's?* Let's be honest, grief can cause logic and reason to take a backseat.

In the thirty-two years since the tragic accident, being a pastor's wife and a minister myself now, I've heard parents who have suffered the same kind of loss, say things like, "I wish I were dead," "You never get over it," "I can't move past it," "If it wasn't for my other children, I'd take a bunch of pills and never wake up." *Was this my aunt and uncle? Did they say these things?* I don't know.

In the world around us, there is no shortage of grief. There is the Surfside condo collapse, a flood that ripped through the streets of Germany, turmoil in South Africa, wildfires in the west, a new Delta variant of the Coronavirus, and a text from my husband with a picture of a kind-hearted young man in our city, an aspiring musician, who was killed in a car accident late one night. *He was just nineteen.* I typed this with tears running down my face. The unexpected text drew me back to the moment I heard the words, "Richard's dead!" My heart hurt for this young man's family, just as it did for mine back then.

This kind-hearted musician named Jacob, whose music we listened to, makes me think of another Jacob, one with twelve sons, who lived thousands of years ago, and whose life and death takes up half of the book of Genesis. Here's a glimpse,

...When he saw the wagons which Joseph had sent to carry him, the spirit of Jacob their father revived.

The writer of Genesis wrote that.

Did you get what the writer was saying? The writer wanted the readers to know that following the death of his favorite son, Jacob lived for twenty-two years in a grief-stricken state, never being fully present for his other sons and family members. This is what Pete Rollins meant by "Trauma steps out of time, and until you heal from the trauma, time can't start back up."

How do I know Jacob lived in a grief-stricken state?

Well, because the writer lets us know that *Jacob's spirit revived.* For something to revive it first must die, or appear dead, anyway. To Jacob, the news of losing his son Joseph became too much. When trauma struck, he became stuck in a state of hopelessness. It wasn't until twenty-two years later, when Jacob heard the news that his son was alive and bore *witness* to it by seeing the wagons which Joseph sent to carry him away on, that his grief was lifted, taken away, carried away. *Gone!*

Grief is a deeply rooted sorrow that is often coupled with despair. Someone said, "Despair is the belief that tomorrow will be an endless repeat of today." *This is true.* Just ask Jacob in the Bible, a child who has lost a parent, a person whose marriage ended, the person who lost their job, the person whose spouse cheated, the person whose reputation was marred by a false accusation, the person who's loved one is addicted to drugs, the person who received a devastating diagnosis, my aunt and uncle, or the person who ate the can of Spaghetti O's.

Grief sits on your chest like a two-ton elephant. It leaves you unable to move, breathe, smile, bathe, eat, or rest. You find yourself wondering, *Will I ever get out from under this weight?* Then you wonder, *Do I even care?* From the epicenter of grief comes blame and regret.

Take for instance these words of Mary...
Lord, if only you had been here my brother would not have died!

Or these words of Adam,
The woman whom you gave to be with me, she gave me fruit of the tree, and I ate![76]

And then I wonder how many times over the twenty-two-year period did Jacob blame himself for sending Joseph off alone to look for his brothers?

Or how many times a parent has said,
"What if I wouldn't have sent her to the store for milk? Then she wouldn't have gone missing."

Or "What if I would have answered the phone? Then they wouldn't have gotten a ride with a stranger. *They would still be here.*"

Or "What if I would have listened to my gut? Then the scammer never would have gotten my bank account information."

Or "What if I would have screamed, and kicked, and fought harder? *They never would have raped me.*"

Or this, What if I would have…*(You fill in the blanks)*

So, what happens when you are no longer knee deep in grief but up to your eyeballs in it? When you can't catch your breath, because nothing is ever going to be the same again? The endless ache of 'what if' feels like your insides are being ripped out and torn to shreds like Joseph's coat of many colors. Reprieve comes only by way of overeating, popping pills, drinking in excess, sex, or sleeping. *Lots of sleeping.*

The answer is forgiveness.

Trust me, I wrestled with these words of Bréne Brown, "Grief is the root of all unforgiveness."[77] I would have liked for her to have explained the statement at the time she said it, but she didn't. So I went toe-to-toe with the Scriptures, pulling out the data and stories in the Bible on grief to see what it had to say about the topic.

What exactly is grief? you ask.

According to David Kessler, a death and grieving expert, it is 'a change that impacts us.' There is *bad* grief and there is *good* grief.

Have you seen the 1989 movie, *National Lampoon's Christmas Vacation* with Chevy Chase? Do you remember the scene where Clark gets trapped in the attic while his family goes off Christmas shopping? He finds an old box of home movies in a wooden trunk. In the very next scene, you hear the flickering of the reel and the song, *The Spirit of Christmas,* by Ray Charles playing in the background. The camera pans over to Clark sitting on the attic floor with his chin in his hands, a wide smile on his face, and one tear rolling down his cheek. He's watching a black-and-white home movie of when he was a boy at Christmas time. Clark is an adult with a wife and kids, yet, the home movie takes him back in time, to when his parents were alive, back to when things were simple and good and safe. And we tear up, because we remember the time when things were simple and good and safe.

There are moments that cause me to miss when my boys were little, when they needed me to tie their shoes, fix their belt, and cut their pancakes, while at the same time celebrating their manhood, of course. Yes, I want them to grow up, and it pains my heart in a good way that they aren't small anymore. Growing up is good and it's a part of life. Rob Bell said in one of his Podcasts, "All change is a form of grief. All grief is loss. All loss needs to be grieved. In order to gain something, you must lose something."[78]

Grief invites you to sit *shiva* in your tears to grieve what *was*, while simultaneously celebrating what *is*. Grief is a pass through—you cry, you laugh, you remember. *But you don't stay there!*

The truth is, we typically think of grief as a *negative* change that impacts us.

Grief is loss.

Loss is pain.

Pain is blame.

The longer you grieve without passing through it, the more pervasive grief becomes, the more bitterness and anger and resentment you heap up, the more blame and anger and pain you project, the more controlling you become, and the more darkness and despair you accumulate.

Are you saying, don't grieve the changes?

Not at all! But I am saying, "Don't set up your tent there!"

Here's why…

At the logging camp, after a hard fifteen-hour day of moving logs downstream, the river drivers would corral the logs in booms at night to keep them from floating away unattended while they ate dinner, mended their socks, greased their cork boots, sang songs, played cards, and slept. Then, at first light, the river drivers would rise, eat a high carb and high protein breakfast, drink a lot of coffee, then head down to the river to open the booms and allow the logs to flow again. They grabbed their pickaroon poles and peavey hooks, jumped in their flat-bottomed wooden boats and started steering the logs downriver to the next logging camp, where the logs again would be held in check by booms overnight. The river drivers repeated this process over and over, from point to point, from logging camp to logging camp, from boom to boom, until the logs finally reached the mill.

On some mornings, the river drivers would go down to the river to release the booms only to discover a log jam had formed overnight. The force of the raging waters flowing beneath the logs bumped and nudged and tossed the thousands of tons of logs around, causing them to pile up and become jammed. The river drivers would have to clear the jam before the logs could flow. This could take hours, a crew of men, and even some dynamite.

The river drivers understood that the logging camps were not a permanent dwelling place and that the booms were not designed to hold the logs long term. *The camps were pass throughs to get them where they're going.*

At the logging camp, there would be a makeshift cabin built from hand cut logs held together by notches. A roof made of hand-cut wood shingles. The spaces between the logs were filled with moss to insulate against the cold. The beds were made of logs and covered with prickly pine boughs. The floors were logs hewed down flat. There was a cookhouse attached to the log cabin, where the wood for the fire, meat, food, and supplies were kept. The ceiling leaked. There were lice in the blankets. There were moose and bears and critters outside. There were no indoor bathrooms, only outhouses. And they didn't see their loved for long periods at a time.[79]

Yes, grief is uncomfortable. *It's meant to be.* Grief is a pass through. Grief has a flow—it should come to us and through us. There are some griefs that stay longer than others. There are griefs that don't flow easily. Some griefs might require you to get up in the morning and clear a log jam or two. Some griefs are expressed in songs sung by the river that become nothing more than songs of sadness when you don't do the work of clearing the log jam. The longer you stay in the camp, the longer you stay emotionally disconnected from your life, the more backed up your logs become in the river of life.

Grief can even become an idol or a god. Here's how.

In his book, "Cup of Salvation," Rabbi Pesach Wolicki explains that the word translated as *sorrow, pain, suffering, toil, or disappointment* in the Hebrew is ETZeV. ETZeV is also the word in Scripture used for *idol*. Rabbi Wolicki says that the word implies, *discomfort*.[80] The reason it implies discomfort is because in ancient times, the people believed that to please the gods they had to cut themselves, inflict pain, and offer sacrifices to the gods. This would mean giving a portion of their crops or offering a child sacrifice. A natural disaster of any kind; a famine, a draught, a crop failure, was seen by the pagans as the gods being angry with them and their solution was to do something that included discomfort in order to please the gods. In their pagan mind, pleasing the gods meant having a balance of sun and rain, good health and weather, and plentiful crops and fatty cattle.[80] Rabbi Wolicki said, "To a pagan mindset it was understood that *to worship meant to give something up* or even *to suffer.*"[81]

So, what happened when pagans sacrificed to make the gods happy, and there was still death and disease and devastation going on all around them? The answer is, they sacrificed more—more cutting, more inflicting pain, more grain offerings, more child sacrifices. Their belief was they hadn't done enough to please the gods, so their response became to give up more, to suffer more.

Prolonged grief becomes something you sacrifice to and suffer for. It's something you offer your time, energy, and attention to, but can't ever satisfy. The grief gods always want more—more discomfort, more suffering, more disconnection. But making grief into an object to be worshipped can't restore what was lost. No amount of pain and discomfort can do that.

When you sabotage the grief process by failing to do the hard work of moving the logs from point to point, logging camp to logging camp, boom to boom, grief becomes a god. When you remain in the same camp over and over—in the same place of discomfort as you were the day before, in the same place of disconnection you were the month before, never coming any closer to reclaiming your life and reconnecting to joy and peace and love, you are making a choice. Each morning you are choosing to lay in the bed of prickly pine boughs to endure more suffering, more discomfort, more disconnection, while you should be opening the booms and releasing the logs.

With grief you have an internal barometer that determines the weight, the length, and the depth of a single loss—no two losses are alike. For example: let's suppose you lose an acquaintance and your internal grief barometer is at 75% for that loss. When you laugh, smile, share a moment of intimacy, or do something that lowers the grief barometer, the instant you catch yourself not *suffering*, you squash the joy and peace and love, and return to the 75%. In doing so, you replace moments of healing with thoughts of anguish and punishment. You tell yourself that *not suffering* is *not remembering*. The more moments of healing you sabotage, the longer you will stay in the place of discomfort and disconnection.

Someone once said, "Your tears water the ground around your feet so that something new can grow."[82] When you hold on to grief, nothing new can grow. Nothing but life choking weeds, that is. Prolonged grief becomes about you, and if you're not careful, you can come to the place where you're no longer mourning the loss, but grief has become your banner.

There's another story in Genesis that I love. God tells Abraham to take his only son, Isaac, and go to the land of Moriah; and offer him as a sacrifice on the mountain that God shall show him.

A bit barbaric. I know!

But what Abraham doesn't say is, "I'll take a rain check."

That's because child sacrifices were a common practice in ancient times. Abraham already knew what to do…he got up early, gathered wood for the burnt offering, prepared his donkey, and made the three-day journey to mount Moriah with his son Isaac and two helpers.

When Abraham sees the mountain in the distance, he tells the two helpers to stay with the donkey, while he and the lad go to worship.

146

Abraham takes the burnt offering, which is Isaac, the wood, and the knife. Together, he and his son make the trek up the mountain.

At a certain point, Isaac asks his father, "Where's the sacrifice?"

To which Abraham responds, "My son, God will provide himself a lamb for a burnt offering."

Isaac seems to be satisfied with that response and keeps walking.

At the top of the mountain, Abraham builds an altar. He lays the wood on it, binds Isaac, and lays him on the wood. Just as he is about to sacrifice his only son, whom he loves, an angel appears. That's when Abraham sees a ram caught in the thicket. It's where God provides a way out for Abraham and a way through for Isaac.

This is a new concept. A God who gives life and doesn't take it. A God who carries away griefs and sorrows. A God who would later come in the form of a Son to lay down His own life just to satisfy His own blood covenant.

God still required the blood of a *son*, just not Isaac's. The ram was a substitute. It was as if God looked back at the Lamb slain from the foundation of the world, and forward to the fullness of time, when He would come to the temple made without hands, made of flesh and blood—a temple that when destroyed would be raised back up in *three* days. The beauty of the Gospel is that Abraham's God, in order to redeem us, took on flesh and blood and became one of us.

Recently, I watched a Tedx Talk by Sarah Montana in Lincoln Square called, "And Why It's Worth It." In her TEDx Talk she shares about forgiving the teenager who killed her mother and brother.[83]

She raised a very good question. "How do you forgive effectively once and for all?"[84]

It's something that Sarah says the Bible doesn't answer.

Or does it?

The Bible tells us to forgive, yet it doesn't give us a nice, neat how-to-guide on how to do it.

But if we look at forgiveness through the lens of a river driver, we might see the question isn't how, but **when**—when the painful, agonizing things that we never wanted to happen gets to the Mill, the Mill Owner will strip the raw timbers of offense down and repurpose them for His glory and for our purpose. Suffering has a way of unveiling purpose, and if we allow it, something beautiful can come from it.

In Sarah's case, she was grieving the loss of her mother and brother and the way her life would have been had they not of been murdered. In my case, I was grieving the loss of my cousin, the loss of my innocence, and the loss of *who* I was before my house was robbed. The resentment and bitterness I was harboring were manifestations of my grief. I wanted my life to return to how it was before Rita opened the Pandora's Box into my past—before the pastor called me vindictive—before my character was assassinated—before I paid twelve-hundred-dollars out-of-pocket to Brother Clay and Brother Aaron—before I ate that can of Spaghetti O's.

Maybe you are grieving *how* things were before the injury, the divorce, the death of the loved one, the affair, the sexual assault, the financial loss, the hurtful accusation, the disfiguring accident, or the destructive thing you said or did and can't take back. Now, your grief manifests itself in an overt way, like through bitterness, resentment, anger, rage, or blame, and is projected onto the very ones you love. When you stay too long, grief mirrors unforgiveness, because grief is the root of all unforgiveness.

It is possible to stay in the same logging camp with your finger on the rewind button replaying the moments leading up to the change *that* changed everything, while becoming more bitter, more resentful, and more disengaged.

Grief creates new normals. Maybe you wouldn't have chosen this for yourself, but there is life on the other side of the loss. The question becomes, *Can you allow grief to be a pass through?*

You are not alone.

The pages of the Bible are filled with river drivers who have been in your cork boots before, who have struggled with loss and blame, and have gone from point to point, logging camp to logging camp, boom to boom, in order to get their *logs* downstream to the place of Completion.

Like who? you ask.

Well, for starters,

There's Job—
A Godly man who lost his children, his possessions, and his health all in the same day, who described the depth of his loss as both anguish and bitterness in his soul.

There's Joseph—
An innocent dreamer who had his special garment stripped from him, who was cast into a pit and sold into slavery by his own brothers, who was falsely accused of rape, who was wrongly imprisoned, and was forgotten by the very one who promised to remember him to Pharaoh.

There's Hannah—
A faithful wife whose grievance was with the LORD, whose heart ached for a child to call her own, who when she prayed, only her lips moved and no words came out.

There's Paul—
The bold mighty evangelist, who was whipped with thirty-nine lashes on five separate occasions by his own people, beaten on three separate occasions with rods, stoned once, shipwrecked, robbed, and falsely accused.

And yet, at the end of their river drive, when the last log reached the Mill, Job received a double restitution, Joseph preserved life, Hannah gave birth to a baby boy, and Paul wrote half of the New Testament. I can only imagine their initial thoughts being, *God doesn't love me! If He did, He wouldn't have allowed this to happen!*

King David said in Psalm 56,
You keep track of all my sorrows. You have collected all my tears in your bottle. You have recorded each one in your book.

This makes me wonder how many bottles the river drivers in the Bible filled with their tears before the Creator of the universe *remembered not to forget* them?

The good news is the God who remembered them, remembers you!

Does this mean that grief will magically vanish?

Nope!

But what if I told you, grief, like *that* hair on the chicken parmesan, doesn't belong to you?

And what if I told you that it's not yours to carry?

Are you serious?
Yes.

How do I know?

Because thousands of years before the birth of Christ, the prophet Isaiah penned,
Surely, he hath borne our griefs, and carried our sorrows.

The Greatest River Driver to ever live uttered three words while suspended from two logs...*It is finished!* These words changed the past, the present, and the future for all humanity. Not only did He come to carry away our sins as the Azazel or Scapegoat, but He came to carry away our griefs and our sorrows, too.

Why?
Because prolonged grief keeps you stuck, and in return, creates distance.

Distance between you and loved ones. Distance between you and joy. Distance between you and peace. Distance between you and love. Distance between you and living. Distance between you and being present. Distance between you and person-to-person relationships.

It's hard to be present when you're hurting. Wouldn't you agree?

The work of Salvation is complete. The Scapegoat came to carry away all things that create distance.

Because grief like Jacob's in the Bible, prevents you from being fully present in your life and in the lives of others. Jesus died so you could live. He died to reclaim your traumas and heal your wounds. He died so time could start back up for you.

God came to reconcile all things to Himself. This includes the distance between you and Him. It may not be possible to get back what you lost, but like Elin Nordegren said after her divorce from Tiger Woods, "Forgiveness takes time. It is the last step of the grieving process."[86]

The good news is there is a place of Completion for your grief, a place where God will repurpose your pain, a place where the worst parts of your story will become the best parts of your story, a place where you will have gained the wisdom to help those whose cork boots you've been in get their logs to the Mill.

But I can't! you say.

Well, then there is another hook I need to introduce you to. One that is used at the mill.

The Cant Hook.

You can't be serious?!
Yes. Yes, I am.

The **Cant Hook**, also called a Cant Dog, looks a lot like the peavey hook with a flat tip, rather than a pointed one. The mouth of the hook is mostly squared with a curve. The Cant Hook was used at the mill to roll the *cant*. A *cant* is a log that has been cut and squared. The Mill Owner used the Cant Hook to hold the *cant* and keep it from moving as he worked on it.[87]

So, if this is you, and grief has separated you from the life you wish to live, the two greatest prayers you can pray are "Help!" and "Here!"

So, go ahead! Cast your cares on Him, because He can't *cant* miss!

He wants all your logs. Even the ones you blame Him for. Just say, "Here!"

Azazel.

Take away.

Scapegoat.

Jesus.

Nasa.

Carry away.

Lift up.

Joseph's wagon.

Clearing a log jam

Photo credit: West Branch Historical Preservation Committee,
http://themaineboomhouses.org/photos-from-the-past/

10

THE KEY LOG

"It's toughest to forgive ourselves. So it's probably best to start with other people. It's almost like peeling an onion. Layer by layer, forgiving others, you really do get to the point where you can forgive yourself"

— Patty Duke

IN THE LIFE of a river driver, an obstruction of any kind, such as a boulder, a fallen tree, a stump, an island in the river, a sudden narrowing of the water way or a shallow riverbed could create a potential log jam. A single log jam could involve hundreds of thousands of logs. If this happened, the river drivers would first try to break up the jam with an axe and a peavey hook, and if that didn't work, they would use dynamite.

Every log jam has a key log.

The *key log* is the log that if removed would free up all the other logs. It's the log that keeps all the other logs *stuck*, causing the water to back up behind it, flooding the surrounding properties and creating potential hazards. The river driver with the most skill and experience was the one whose job it was to inspect the jam and locate the key log. Once it was located, a dynamite charge would be tied to a pole and inserted behind the key log. The fuse on the dynamite pack would burn under the water long enough for the experienced river driver to take cover. The explosion would send entire logs and debris into the air freeing the key log, thus, allowing all the other logs to flow freely again.[88]

The original sin, also called the ancestral sin or the inherited sin, is said to be passed down through the male bloodline and has existed since Adam and Eve's disobedience in the garden, when they ate of the tree of the knowledge of good and evil. As a result of Adam's disobedience, sin entered the world.

The Apostle Paul writes about the ancestral sin in Romans 5, and says this,
Wherefore, as by one man sin entered into the world, and death by sin; and so death passed upon all men, for that all have sinned:

Universally speaking, the Original Sin is the Key Log—*it's the log that if removed would free up all the other logs.* Jesus came that we might have life and life more abundantly. For more than fifteen hundred years, from Mount Sinai to the destruction of the second temple, Israel's high priest would rehearse the annual Day of Atonement, a feast designed to roll their sins ahead for another year, in anticipation of that *which is to come,* not realizing the Messiah King had already come in the form of a Son. A Son that Paul refers to as the Second Adam. The Second Adam came to reverse the curse placed on mankind in the garden and to free up the universal key log that originated with Adam and Eve four-thousand years ago.

In Genesis 3, we read about a series of curses placed on the man, the woman, and the devil. God told the serpent, which is the devil, this,
I will put enmity between thee and the woman, and between thy seed and her seed; it shall bruise thy head, and thou shalt bruise his heel.

I love this—
Sandwiched between fig aprons and animal skins is where we find the first promise of the Redeemer. **Blood had to be shed. Something had to die.** The covering that God made of animal skins was temporal and could not take away their sin. But, the Lamb slain from the foundation of the world could, and later, would.

From the very beginning, the Hebrew Scripture testifies that the Messiah would triumph over the devil. Hope isn't an emotion. It is a state of being. In the garden, God planted a seed of *hope* in the heart of the man and the woman for the struggle to come. A hope that is deeply rooted in all of us still today.

As Ray Vander Laan explains, the Septuagint contains the earliest Greek translation of the Hebrew Scriptures, which was most likely used by the Greek speaking Jews in Egypt. He says that when you read the David and Goliath story in the Septuagint, the writer uses numbers to convey a message about Goliath to his Jewish audience—Goliath was **six** cubits tall, his armor weighed **six thousand** shekels, and his spear point weighed **six hundred** shekels.[89]

666

Did you catch that?

But that's not all. The writer adds this,
His armor looked like scales.

To the Jewish audience, the repeated use of the number *six* would imply Goliath is evil, and by comparing his armor to scales, the writer is making the comparison to a snake.

Where do we first read about a snake?

Correct. In the garden of Eden.

The writer wants us to know that the descendant of Eve has bruised the head of the snake. It's a very creative way of rehearsing the Creation account and giving hope to the hearers. The writer that captures the story of David and Goliath in the book of I Kings is Jewish. His audience is Jewish. He's pointing the people back to the garden of Eden, back to the story of Adam and Eve, back to the writings of Moses, back to the promise that 'the seed of a woman will crush the head of the serpent.' The writer wants them to know that, 'The Hebrew Scripture is true. And just as the descendant of Eve bruised the head of the snake, when Messiah comes, He will do the same.'

The Gospel of John borrows themes and concepts from the writings of Moses, which we know as the first five books of the Bible, also known as the Torah in the Hebrew or the Pentateuch in the Greek and reinterprets them in light of Jesus Christ.

Here's one:
And as Moses lifted up the serpent in the wilderness, even so must the Son of man be lifted up:

Here's another:
In the beginning was the word, and the word was with God, and the word was God.

And another:
Behold, the Lamb of God, which takes away the sin of the world.

John is Jewish. He has an agenda. He wants the Jewish people to see that Jesus Christ is the embodiment of the Torah. He wants the people to make the connection between the first promise of the Redeemer in the garden, and Jesus being the fulfillment of that promise.

Notice in the verse above how John doesn't say, *sins*. He says *sin*. If we were to translate this into river driver's language, it would read, "Look! The River Driver, which takes away the key log of the world."

In 2005, ABC News reported that the blood of a sheep in South Australia was being used to provide the anti-venom used for rattlesnake bites.[90]

Hmm.

This isn't new news. Two-thousand years ago, the blood of a spotless lamb was used to reverse the effects of the snake bite in the garden.

On the cross, the Greatest River Driver to ever live, uttered three words that changed the past, the present, and the future for all mankind—*It is finished*. Before Adam ever sinned, before heaven and earth was ever created, before the first star was ever hung, God made a way of escape for us. That way being Jesus Christ, the Chief Corner Stone, and the Lamb slain from the foundation of the world. He came into the world to crush the head of the devil, once and for all.

The New Testament teaches that when Jesus died, He went down to hell to take back the keys of hell that the devil stole in the garden of Eden. He spent three days and nights in the heart of the earth, preaching to the spirits/souls there.

Hell is the place where souls go to wait for the final resurrection and judgment and is divided into two parts—paradise and the bottomless pit. These two parts are said to be separated by a great divide.

In the story of Jonah, the belly of the whale symbolizes the tomb, the grave, and the place of waiting for the dead, or simply put, hell.

Let's not forget that in Chapter four, we discussed how that the book of Jonah uses Jewish words and concepts to suggest that the prophet died.

Hell is oftentimes thought of as "The Land of Forgetfulness," and yet the Hebrew Scripture describes Jonah's prayers on the third day as coming up before the LORD into the holy temple. If Jonah died, which is plausible, then even in death Jonah couldn't have escaped God, because his prayers, like all the prayers of the saints mentioned in the book of Revelation, come up before the throne as incense and are collected in golden bowls. The Scripture teaches in Psalms that if we make our bed in *hell*, God is there. The same was true for Jonah. And then, when you consider the Jewish literature and funeral practices which teach that the soul of a deceased person hovers over the body for three days intending to reenter it—you have the corpse of Jonah being spit out on the third day, and his soul reentering the body, when God said, "Cumi."

But wait!—There's more!

The Jewish people read the book of Jonah every year on the Day of Atonement with the belief that there are certain severities to sin. Depending on the severity of their sin, it may come with capital punishment, which is, to say, death. According to Jewish tradition, the violation of a Mitzvah (law) can only be atoned for through the death of the individual, which is why Jewish commentaries teach that Aaron's two sons, Nadab and Abihu, died on the Day of Atonement.[91]

Just one more thing…

Consider the acid in the whale's stomach. It's likely that it would have bleached the pigment in Jonah's skin, perhaps even dissolving the hair on his body. Now picture this, a bald prophet, who is white as a ghost, appearing in Nineveh.

Jonah in his resurrected body.
Jesus in His.

Hmm.

John writes,
Verily, verily, I say unto you, except a corn of wheat fall into the
ground and die, it abideth alone: but if it die, it bringeth forth much
fruit.

What John is saying is something had to die, so that something could
live.

What happened after Jonah was resurrected?

Nineveh repented.

When something happens twice in Scripture, for example, Pharaoh
dreaming the two dreams and Joseph interpreting them both as one,
it is a very Jewish way of saying that it is from God. The *first*
symbolizes the natural. The *second* symbolizes the spiritual. Which
is why Nicodemus, who happens to be very Jewish, and is a leader
of the Jews, asks Jesus this question, "How can a man be born when
he is old? Can he enter the second time into his mother's womb, and
be born?"

To which Jesus answers,
Except a man be born of water and of the Spirit, he cannot enter into
the kingdom of God. That which is born of the flesh is flesh; and that
which is born of the Spirit is spirit. Marvel not that I said unto thee,
Ye must be born again.

Paul says this about the first Adam,
Therefore as by the offence of one judgment came upon all men to
condemnation;

And this about the second,
even so by the righteousness of one the free gift came upon all men unto justification of life.

Acts 1:8 says,
Ye shall receive power, after the Holy Ghost is come upon you...

The word *power* in the Greek is the word *dunamis.* It's where we get the word dynamite from.

Jesus is the new Adam. He died and went into the heart of the earth to take back the keys of death and hell, which were taken when sin intruded upon the world when the first Adam sinned. He died and went into the heart of the earth to give us the power to break up key logs in our own hearts and minds through the power of the Holy Ghost.

It's essential to know that a log jam can have more than one key log. Jesus took care of the universal key log, which is, the original sin, and has left us with the *dunamis* power to pry apart and blast apart all the other key logs holding us back and keeping us stuck physically, spiritually, and emotionally. Namely unforgiveness, which masquerades as anger, criticism, bitterness, resentment, shame, and grief. Unforgiveness restricts the flow of the Spirit in our everyday life. Let's look at two very specific key logs, *shame* and *grief,* to see how they hold us back and keep us stuck in unforgiveness.

THE KEY LOG: SHAME

A year after my cousin, Richard, died, I moved to Newport News, Virginia, to be with my parents and to serve in the church. From the time I was baptized at the age of fourteen, I lived, breathed, and dreamed church. I didn't curse or use vulgar words like "shut-up" or "fart." I didn't use drugs, smoke cigarettes, or drink alcohol. I stopped wearing pants, jewelry, and make-up. I stopped cutting my hair, listening to rock and roll music, and going to the school dances. Instead, I prayed, fasted, volunteered for the bus ministry, taught Bible studies, sang in the choir, and was a well-known Bible Quiz champion. I memorized large portions of the Bible, even whole books, and quizzed against other teams from all fifty states and Canada. I was by all standards—a very good girl, and upon my up-and-coming high school graduation, I planned to attend Kent Christian College.

But no matter how good I appeared to be; deep down inside, I knew I was flawed. I was a bad person. A sinner with a secret. And if the church knew who I really was deep down inside, they would separate themselves from me.

My fall from grace happened when I was seventeen and the pastor found out that my boyfriend and I were having sex. The pastor said, "I'm disappointed in you, Francine." Hearing his words made me shrink with shame. *If he was disappointed, then how much more was God disappointed in me?* The pastor removed me from the choir, the bus ministry, and the Bible Quiz Team.

Ever since I could remember, sex equaled love and belonging. The flaw had been put there when I was six, by my uncle, and by the time I was seventeen, it was intricately woven into the fabric of my being. I didn't know how to rid myself of it. It felt like my prayers to conquer fornication once and for all fell on deaf ears. That God, like the pastor, didn't have any more grace for me. It didn't take long before my secret was out to the whole church, and the ones I trusted the most shunned, judged, and gossiped about me.

I wrestled with Paul's words, *O wretched man that I am, who shall deliver me from the body of this death.* Shame magnified my loneliness, and the church felt like a barren and graceless place. I went from worshipping on the front row to hiding on the back row.

I allowed the words "I'm disappointed in you" to cause me to shrink with shame and rob me of my self-worth.

Until recently, I chalked up my lack of risk taking to being reserved. But there's something Brené Brown said in her book *Daring Greatly* that makes me think otherwise, "Shame has two tapes: *I'm not enough* and *Who do you think you are?*"[92] I realized after reading her book that those two tapes run through my mind a lot. What I didn't realize was that almost every layer of vulnerability was underpinned by shame.

But shame isn't a new struggle. It's been around since before Moses wore knee-pants. Not only did sin enter the world in the garden, but shame entered holding its hand.

Here, see for yourselves.
*and Adam and his wife **hid themselves** from the presence of the LORD God amongst the trees of the garden.*

Moses wrote that, and this,
*And the LORD God called unto Adam, and said unto him, Where art thou? And he said, I heard thy voice in the garden, and I was **afraid**, because I was **naked**...*

And then he wrote this,
*Therefore the LORD God sent him forth from the garden of Eden, to till the ground from whence he was taken. **So he drove out the man**...*

The first time I heard the difference between guilt and shame explained in a way that made sense was when Sheila Walsh was discussing her battle with depression on the 700 Club. She said, "Shame is when you are something wrong. Guilt is when you did something wrong."[93]

In Brené Brown's research on shame and vulnerability, she defines shame as "the intensely painful feeling or experience of believing that we are flawed and therefore unworthy of love and belonging – something we've experienced, done, or failed to do makes us unworthy of connection."[94] In the book, she includes a quote by her friend Robert Hilliker that says, "Shame started as a two person experience, but as I got older, I learned how to do shame all by myself."[95]

Shame condemns you and holds you captive. But grace is the opposite. It's the absence of condemnation.

Edward T. Welch said, "Shame is life-dominating and stubborn. Once it enters your heart and mind, it is a squatter that refuses to leave."[96]

So then, how do you get rid of shame?

That's a good question, which I'll get to in a minute. But first, what I thought was shyness is *really* shamefulness, a pervasive form of unworthiness. In my twenties, I dreaded going out alone. When I did, I walked with my head down to avoid the furrowed brows, the awkward stares, and the eye-rolling-*thing* that happens at the grocery store, in the hallway, at the park, and in general, the once-over given to determine how pretty, how rich, how intelligent, how good, and how important you are. I've progressed over the years, but the struggle with shame is *still* real for me. My husband is my first line of defense against my deeply rooted sense of unworthiness, but he probably has no idea to what extent.

At one time, I would have waited on him to open a public door for me, not in some gentlemanly fashion way, but because I wasn't sure whether to pull or to push, or to push or to pull, and I didn't want to be seen pulling when I should have been pushing, pushing when I should have been pulling, and to avoid the obscure chance that someone might laugh at me, I would stand back and let him go first.

Shame is painful and deeply personal on every level. When I was eleven and my uncle went to jail for sexually abusing me, my aunt, who lived next door, started calling me names, like "floozy-Suzy" and "trouble-maker with a capital 'T'." For months she made it her mission to berate me and tell me that "I got what I deserved" and that "my uncle gave me what I asked for." Between the sexual abuse, my aunt's constant shaming, and my parents' inability to express affection and affirmation in the way that I needed them to, I became an expert at doing shame all by myself. And when I was raped at twelve-years old by a thirty-eight-year-old stranger in the woods, I told myself that "I asked for it!" that "I deserved it!" that "I was a floozy-Suzy!" After the event in the woods, I became more aggressive and unpredictable. My sisters feared me, my parents didn't know what to do with me, and I found myself searching for love, even when I had to go through the mud to get it.

There's a story in the Bible of a woman caught in adultery, taken in the very act. *Eight* accusers dragged her through the streets to the temple, where Jesus was teaching, and tossed her down, naked, or close to it. In this story, Jesus uses the peavey hook to silence her accusers. The accusers were a group of religious Pharisees, leaders of the Jewish people. Back then, the Pharisees followed one of two teachings, Hillel or Shammai, the two great scholars of that time. Hillel taught that the commandment "Love your neighbor" took priority over "adultery," while Shammai taught that the commandment "do not commit adultery" took priority over "love thy neighbor." So, depending on which teacher they adhered to, determined whether they should *let her go* or *stone her*.

There are endless speculations as to what Jesus may have written with His finger in the dust, to which nobody can be sure. But what we do know is that as a Rabbi, Jesus would have used word pictures and imagery to point the accusers to the text to answer for themselves whether they should stone her. One speculation is that Jesus wrote the names of her accusers in the dust as to intentionally draw their thoughts to the very specific passage in Jeremiah 17, where it says that anyone who forsakes the LORD will have their names written in the earth, and that He gives to every man according to the fruit of his doings.

Here, read for yourself. Verses 10 and 13,
The LORD searches the hearts, and tries the reigns, and gives to every man according to his ways, and according to the fruit of his doings...All that forsake me shall be ashamed, and they that depart from me shall be written in the earth.

The Pharisees wanted the woman to be condemned to death. But Jesus turned it over. What began with *eight* accusers ended as a new beginning for the woman. The "no condemnation" part came before the "Go and sin no more" part.

Which brings me back to the thought that shame condemns the place in which it squats. The way to get rid of shame is to silence the accuser. If there is no accuser, there is no condemnation. If there is no condemnation, there is no shame. To eliminate shame, it is important to turn the offense over and look at it through the lens of empathy, compassion, and understanding.

Mike Meadows said, "Unforgiveness is when you freezeframe someone in their weakness."[97]

This is very true!

It doesn't have to be another person that we freeze-frame, it can be us ourselves.

In order to eradicate shame, you need to extend empathy not just to others, but also to yourself.

Here are some steps to remove the key log of shame in your life:

1. Forgive yourself for all the things you had to do to survive.
2. Speak to yourself with the same level of compassion you would speak to someone else.
3. Don't believe everything you think.
4. Give yourself the gift of affirmation. The daily practice of you telling yourself all the things that you wished you heard while growing up.
5. Stop hiding behind masks. You are enough!
6. Use your voice to shed light on the shadows and expose the secrets that have kept you stuck in the pain of your past.
7. Stop holding yourself to a higher standard than you hold others to.

The Greatest River Driver to ever live endured the humiliation of the cross so that you could live without condemnation. As a river driver your main job is to prevent log jams and to get the logs to the Mill. If you have a log jam, then you've got to find the key log, and remove it before the logs can flow again. We've talked about ways to identify shame and how to heal from it, now let's talk about another key log, one that is equally as menacing, grief.

THE KEY LOG: GRIEF

Not only did shame enter the world holding hands with sin, but grief entered holding sin's other hand. Shame and grief are different sides of the same coin. Both keep you stuck. Both are key logs. Shame counts the 'what if's' before the loss, while grief counts the 'what if's' after the loss. Shame romanticizes what is down the road, while grief romanticizes what is in the rear-view mirror. Grief creates distance, and there's Scripture for it:

Therefore the LORD *God sent him forth from the garden of Eden, to till the ground from whence he was taken.* ***So he drove out the man****...*

Moses wrote that.

Remember this? Grief is loss. Loss is pain. Pain is blame. Well, from the very beginning, we see grief fast at work. First, we see it in the amount of loss suffered in the garden: loss of innocence, loss of relationship with the Creator, loss of their home, loss of their homeland, loss of their food source, and loss of their lifestyle. Second, we see it in the blame and the finger pointing. Eve blames the devil, and Adam blames both the woman and the Creator. Third, we see it in the curses, curses that include pain and sorrow and difficulty.

Grief keeps its eyes in the rearview mirror. 'What if I didn't visit that tree?' 'What if I didn't listen to the serpent?' 'What if I didn't desire to be like God and know good from evil?' 'What if I didn't offer Adam a bite?' 'What if I didn't forget the commandment of the LORD?' 'What if we would have said sorry, rather than place blame?' *Things might have turned out differently.*

Grief, as we learned in Chapter 9, is a change that impacts us. We see this in the garden. The man and the woman were forbidden to reenter Eden, lest at any time, they eat of the Tree of Life and live forever in a sinful state. The Bible records that Adam lived 930 years. How many times in those 930 years do you think Adam revisited *that* day in his mind? How many times in those 930 years do you think the two tapes of shame played in his head: "You're not enough" and "Who do you think you are?" Every morning when Adam opened his eyes, he opened them to another wave of grief washing over him, reminding him that he was *that* Adam...The one who ushered sin into the world...The one who lost two sons in one day, one to murder and one to banishment.

As stated previously, we can spend a lifetime with our finger on the rewind button replaying the moments leading up to the change *that* changed everything. One Sunday, a young woman in my church ran over to me and threw her head down in my lap and cried. She had lost her father when she was very young, and from that moment on, she felt unloved, unwanted, and invisible to her mother and to her eleven siblings. She is the baby of the family and was daddy's little princess. Without him there to affirm these things in her, she feels the daily absence of beauty and the ever-encroaching presence of torment and anguish. She's been clutching grief for so long that it affects her health and wellbeing on every level. As I prayed with her, I told her, "It's time to forgive your daddy for leaving you. It's time to forgive him for dying. It's time to forgive all the hurts, real and perceived." It sounds silly, but it is a real thing. We can romanticize the loss and hold onto the pain and blame, until it destroys us. I told her that grief was her key log and that Jesus came to carry her griefs away.

The following week, I had her write a letter to her mother (a letter that would not be mailed). She told her mother how she felt unloved, unwanted, and emotionally abandoned ever since her dad passed. She wrote how that she longed for her mother to tell her, "I love you," and wished for her to wrap her arms around her. She wrote how she feels bad about herself and that she was angry with her mother. Because the last time she went home to visit, she didn't receive any affection or hear any affirmations. She's angry because all the signposts seem to confirm that she's not worthy of love and belonging.

Then, I had her write a second letter. This time, the assignment was to put herself in her mother's shoes and write a letter back to herself. *Make sure you put her shoes on,* I said. *What would your mother say to what you wrote? How would your mother feel after reading it?* These are the things I asked her to consider. Why? *Because there are two sides to every story.* I told her to fight with empathy and to use the peavey hook to see it through her mother's eyes. *Your mother may have no idea you feel this way. She can't read your mind,* I said to her, *so if you've never expressed it, then she might be totally oblivious to your expectations and wants.* Then I told her this, "All a grown up really is is a child trapped in an adult sized body."[98] I wanted her to see the little girl trapped inside her mother's skin. To see the pain of her mother's childhood. To see the pain of her mother's loss when her husband died and left her to fend for their children. To see the anger and the fear her mother felt. To extend compassion and understanding to those places. To sit *shiva* with her in her grief because suffering has a way of blurring the lines and bringing the Holy down. Because, like the blue string, suffering unites. It's then that, she would finally be able to free herself of the key log *grief,* which is the root of all unforgiveness. From which comes the shoots of shame.

But why a letter? you ask.

Because it's a tangible way to release pain and because words have power. Every time God spoke in Genesis chapter one something grew. And because pain is the origin of suffering. If there is no pain, then there is no need for person-to-person forgiveness.

Having said that, any area in which you experience pain should be identified as an area that needs forgiveness. *Even if the pain is minimal?* you ask. Yes! Even if the pain is minimal. It's the little foxes that spoil the vine. Which is why God wants all your logs. Identify and localize the source of your pain and apply the healing power of forgiveness before it turns into an infection and spreads.

The truth of the matter is, it's hard to be present when we're hurting. This applies physically, emotionally, spiritually, and psychologically. Consider how when someone is hurting physically, say, *sciatica,* the pain they experience in their body may manifest as anger, cynicism, hypersensitivity, moodiness, rudeness, self-harm, impatience, and sleeplessness, to name a few. Well, the same is true emotionally, spiritually, and psychologically. Pain is pain, and it all manifests the same.

When taking communion, Paul writes in I Corinthians 11,
So anyone who eats this bread or drinks this cup of the Lord **unworthily** *is guilty of sinning against the body and blood of the Lord.*[99]

It's Paul's usage of the word *unworthily* that draws my attention back to the definition of *worthiness* in Brené Brown's book, *The Gifts of Imperfection*. She writes, "Wholehearted living is about engaging in our lives from a place of **worthiness**. It means cultivating the courage, compassion, and connection to wake up in the morning and think, 'No matter what gets done and how much is left undone, I am enough.' It's going to bed at night thinking, 'Yes, I am imperfect and vulnerable and sometimes afraid, but that doesn't change the truth that I am also brave and worthy of love and belonging."[100]

To add onto that, it is taking the cup and the bread of the Lord from a place of worthiness. Knowing wholeheartedly that we are worthy of love and belonging, not because of anything we've done, but because of what Christ did, though we may come from very different places, we have all been given a seat at the Lord's table, to eat bread continually, as a son, and as a daughter.

In the book *Daring Greatly*, Brown divided the men and woman she had interviewed into two groups, those that felt worthy of love and belonging, and those that didn't. Here's what she found:

"Those who feel a deep sense of love and belonging, and those who struggle for it—there's only one variable that separates the groups: Those who feel lovable, who love, and

who experience belonging simply believe they are worthy of love and belonging."[101]

These words on wholehearted living makes me think about the communion cup a little bit differently. Doesn't it you? Paul's words to not eat the bread and drink the cup of the Lord unworthily has more to do with how we view ourselves, whether we believe we are worthy of love and belonging, and not whether we are tithe paying members, or said a curse word that morning, or yelled at our kids on the way to church. What Paul is saying is, come to the table knowing who you are in Christ. Come with the confidence that the God of heaven knew you from your mother's womb and prepared a place *just* for you.

What does this have to do with forgiveness? you ask.

Everything!

When we forget the dead, they die twice. The beauty of the Gospel is that, when we remember Christ and His suffering—the past becomes the present, and the blue string that wraps around all the other strings makes us one through forgiveness in His name, through the power in His blood, through the glory in His resurrection. Forgiveness is the purest form of love. *It casts out all fear.*

The second Adam came to restore *shalom* which was disrupted in the garden. Shalom is the Hebrew word for peace, but it means much more than that. It's also wholeness, completeness, and the absence of chaos or war. Both inwardly and outwardly.

Isaiah writes,
But he was wounded for our transgressions, he was bruised for our iniquities: the chastisement of our peace was upon him; and with his stripes we are healed.

Transgressions and iniquities are not the same thing. One is inward and one is outward. A transgression has to do with an intentional violation of trust and is considered an outward sin or a wound. While iniquity refers to the deceitfulness of a person's heart and is considered an inward sin or a bruise.

The chastisement of our peace was upon Him—

Do you see how huge this is?

The Messiah was *wounded* for our outward sins and *bruised* for our inward sins. Jesus died so that He could save every part of us. That includes, body, mind, and spirit. He died so that we could have wholeness and completeness and live without chaos. It is by His stripes that we have perfect peace, completeness, wholeness, and forgiveness. The Peace of God is transformational and goes beyond human understanding.

Jesus told His disciples,

Peace I leave with you, my peace I give unto you: not as the world giveth, give I unto you…

In the Scriptures leading up to this, Jesus tells His disciples that He must go away, so that He can return in a new form, which we know as the Holy Ghost. The Holy Ghost is *dunamis* power and it searches our hearts for key logs to break up, to blast apart the log jams that hold us back and keep us stuck. Shame and grief are two key logs that lead to rejection, fear, bitterness, and anger, to name a few.

Is shame or grief or both holding you back from love, joy, and peace?

Shame is a squatter, grief is a robber, and both are key logs that entered the world with the original sin. The good news is that from the same hill, from the same cross, from the same place that suffering came, forgiveness freely flows, and this can be you. God wants all your logs.

VULNERABILITY AND FORGIVENESS

River drivers were risk takers! Their work required that they get the logs to the mill, and that's just what they did—rain or shine, snow or ice, calm streams or raging rapids—the river drivers ran, balanced, and jumped over slippery wet logs, day after day, week after week, month after month, for as long as it took to reach the mill. They were resilient, strong, quick footed, and agile. The cork boots with the spiked leather heels helped them stand firm on floating logs and secured their footing against the elements.

As a river driver, we must be willing to take risks—emotional risks, that is, to get our *logs* to the Mill for God to repurpose them on purpose and for His purpose. That means showing up in the turbulent and rocky waters with our pickaroon poles and peavey hooks in hand and our cork boots laced up and ready to go, not knowing what the outcome will be.

There's a story Ruth Graham Lotz shared at Liberty University of a boy who wanted to go to the circus, but whose father couldn't afford to buy tickets. So, as a surprise, the father worked extra hours, and when the day came, he gave the boy one ticket and explained it was all he could afford and that he would have to go alone. The boy took the ticket and headed to Main Street to watch the elephants, and the horses, and the clowns exit the train and parade past him on the street…

> While he stood on the curb, a clown came over and stuck out his hand and the boy gave him his ticket. The clown took the ticket and went on his way, and the little boy was thrilled.

Afterward, the boy told his father all about it. "You won't believe the big elephant and the fancy horses with the dancing girls and the dogs wearing tutus and walking on their hind legs," he said.

"Wow!" the father replied, "what did you think of the trapeze artist and the lion that jumped through the hoop of fire?"

"I didn't see anything like that," the boy said.

"Well, what did you see? Didn't you go into the big tent?" the father asked.

"What tent?" the boy said.

"The tent at the end of the street," the father replied.

"No," the boy said.

"Well then, you never went to the circus. You just watched the parade go by."[102]

We do this all the time, don't we?

Watch the parade go by. Like in worship service, when everyone is dancing and going in, and we're watching from our seat, when everything in us wants to join the celebration, but the skin we're in keeps us stuck. One thing I've learned is that almost every layer of vulnerability is underpinned by shame. But vulnerability doesn't feel so scary when you know the real culprit is *shame*.

Back when my husband was an infant, before seat belts and car seats were mandatory, his mother was holding him in the front passenger seat when the car they were in was involved in an accident. His mother held him tightly as her head hit the windshield and shards of glass penetrated her face. His mother was taken to the hospital, where the emergency room doctor plucked out the shards of glass one by one with tweezers.

Nine years later, a painful lump formed on her forehead and his mother could feel something sharp in the center of it. The lump swelled and oozed, until a shard of glass worked its way out.

This is us. Just when we think we've healed; another shard of shame appears.

Something else Brené Brown said, is that we use the "fear of vulnerability as an armor we put on to protect ourselves against pain, rejection, grief, fear, and disappointment. The only problem is, we can't selectively protect against these emotions without also keeping out joy and love and peace."[103]

It's so true! We protect ourselves against the negative emotions, so that we don't get wounded, not realizing that we obstruct the flow of joy and love and peace in our life.

There's a Jewish wedding practice that I love. It's where the bride circles the groom seven times on their wedding day. The seven circles symbolize the seven times the Jewish people circled the walls of Jericho and how that on the seventh time, the walls came tumbling down. The "walls" symbolize our vulnerability.[104]

But before we delve into the Jewish wedding practice, there are a few things you should know about Jericho, the priests blowing their shofars, and the Israelite men shouting with their voices that you probably didn't learn in Sunday School. First, Rosh Hashanah is the Jewish New Year. In ancient times, it was known as Yom Teruah or the Feast of Trumpets. It is the sacred day of blowing the shofar, which is the ram's horn. Rosh Hashanah is a fall feast and is the fifth feast on the Jewish religious calendar. To this day, the Jewish people still gather at the synagogue with their shofars to blow 100 shofar blasts in unison and make noise.

In the Bible, the commandment to blow the shofar can be found in the Torah, in the books of Leviticus and Numbers, to be exact. Of the 100 blasts from the shofar, some are short broken-sounding blasts, while others are long-sounding blasts, where the note is held out. The short broken-sounding blast resembles a cry, while the longer blast is said to resemble a wailing woman or someone travailing in need.

The second thing is that the ram's horn dates all the way back to Abraham and Isaac, to the ram caught in the thicket. In Jewish tradition, it is said that Abraham bound Isaac on the Feast of Trumpets. The rabbis teach that on Rosh Hashanah, when they blow the shofar that God moves from a seat of judgment to a seat of mercy and forgiveness. The blowing of the shofar reminds God of His covenant with Israel.[105]

Let me diverse for a moment. I learned recently that the word *vulnerability* comes from the Latin word *vulnerare*, meaning "to wound."[106]

Profound, huh?

It reminds me of the words Isaiah penned in chapter 53,
But He was wounded...

Christ was wounded for us.

On the Jewish religious calendar, there is a ten-day period between New Year's Day and the Day of Atonement. These ten days are known as "The Days of Awe." The Days of Awe is a time of repentance and self-reflection. It is a time when the Jewish people examine their deeds for any wrongdoings that they might have committed during the prior year. It's a time of reconciliation when they go to someone they wronged and apologize. It is also a time when the people pay back any money they owe and return any property that doesn't belong to them. Collectively, during the ten days of Awe, the Jewish people do whatever is necessary to make things right with God and with their fellow people.[107]

To the Jewish people, the Day of Atonement is not only the annual day of rolling their sins ahead for another year, but it is also a day of grafting and re-grafting. Meaning, that if the person feels cut off from the presence of God due to some shortcoming or wrongdoing, they can be grafted back in on this day.[108]

What is even more interesting is that when a farmer grafts a tree, he first cuts a shoot off one tree and makes an incision in another tree and then slides the shoot into the incision.

Did you catch that?

The farmer wounds *both* trees.

The word *decision* comes from the Latin word *decidere*.[109] The root word *cis* means "to cut off." This is where we get the English word for scissors, incision, precision, and many more. When we decide something, we are removing, detaching, cutting off all other choices, options, or routes.

To make-a-decision is to make-a-cut.

So, essentially, when we decide to cut off the negative emotions by walling ourselves in to protect against pain, rejection, grief, fear, and disappointment, we are making the decision to cut ourselves off from the good emotions, like joy and peace and love.

The shofar is an instrument used to make noise and resembles the sound of crying. But get this—the human voice is also an instrument used to make noise to God. The Book of Psalms tells us to shout unto God with the voice of triumph.

Back at the battle of Jericho, the priests blew their shofars and the men shouted with their voices before the walls came down. Well, when we cry out to God with our voice, He hears our cry, and moves from a seat of judgment to a seat of mercy and forgiveness.

NOW LET'S GO back to the Jewish wedding practice, to the bride who circles the groom seven times. This is a beautiful picture of what it means to be fully vulnerable. A way to say without words, *I trust you with my whole being. Now trust me with yours.* Someone who has been abused may find it especially difficult to open up. But, vulnerability is a necessary element in cultivating healthy relationships. The walls of vulnerability get wider, higher, and more difficult with time. Keep in mind, everyone and everything you need is on the other side of that wall.

My husband is a full-on extrovert and people person. He has more energy than the electric company. He's a brilliant preacher and a master storyteller. There's nothing he won't do to make someone laugh or to get his point across—sing, dance, roll on the floor. He preaches from a place of humility and vulnerability that is unprecedented. He's the most beautiful human being I know. Love, affirmation, and joy naturally flow from him. He's someone who listens intently and makes you feel important and loved—no matter who you are, no matter where you are, if you are in the presence of William Westgate—you are loved!

But it's never been that easy for me. It takes a lot to make me laugh. I mean, truly laugh, the kind that starts in the pit of your belly and works its way up and out with uncontainable tears and unstoppable squeals. When I finally do laugh like that, it's as though a *key log* has been broken up and all the joy and love and peace that had been kept back comes flooding out in a soul cleansing way.

Yet, it wasn't until after I had a judgment free and honest conversation with my husband that I realized I was "situationally vulnerable." Here's what I mean by that. Certain things were easy for me to express, while other things were merely impossible, like saying, "I love you" and dolling out hugs and kisses to my boys. *I wasn't always like that with my boys.*

During that difficult conversation, I realized that when my boys turned six years of age, the age I was when my uncle began abusing me, a wall went up. Literally—trauma stepped out of time and until I healed from it, time couldn't start back up. My subconscious correlated their being six years of age to my being six years old. Suddenly, the walls I built to protect myself from pain, rejection, grief, fear, and disappointment as a child, were now keeping out joy and love and peace as an adult.

To add to that, I grew up in a household where love and affirmation didn't flow, it trickled. My siblings and I knew our parents loved us, because that's what parents do. They love their children. But, they didn't say it and didn't show it, except for once in a blue moon. What we did receive on a regular basis was name-calling, "Ding-dong," "Dim-Witt," "Knuckle-head," "Nimrod," coupled with "Get out of the way! You ain't a window!" "Move it or lose it!" or "Use your noggin for something other than a hat rack, gal."

Coming back to what Dr. Phil said, "Whoever said, 'Time heals all wounds,' lied. It's what you do with the time that heals the wounds."

Healing comes in small moments, and that conversation with my husband was one of those moments. I was faced the decision to "bring the walls down" or to "keep them up."

With short broken-sounding blasts and long-drawn-out blasts, I made my *decision*. And with that decision,

I sobbed,

I cried,

I wailed,

I repented,

and the walls came down. The strange thing was, it wasn't God this time that moved from a seat of judgment to a seat of mercy and forgiveness, it was me! Suddenly, the words "I forgive you, Francine," swept over my soul like a fire tornado as I forgave myself for all the things I had to do to survive. It was then I decided that I wasn't going to stand on the curb any longer. I wanted in the *big top!*

Vulnerability is more than the sum total of negative emotions. It is the sum total of all emotions belonging to the human experience— it's the good and the bad, the dark and the light, the negative and the positive. Though the details with your story might be different, the walls are the same. It's never too late for the walls of vulnerability that you erected to protect yourself to come down. All it takes is one decision. One broken cry. Because like Mike Norton said, "Few suffer more than those who refuse to forgive themselves."[110]

So, go ahead, give it a try. Or should I say, a cry.

Jesus can't *cant* miss!

IS GUILT A KEY LOG?
Yes and no. Guilt oftentimes is the primary effect or the root cause of something, which is to say, the wound or the opening, while shame and grief are the secondary effects of the primary, which is to say, it's the bacteria that enters the body through the wound and causes infection to spread through the tissue and bloodstream. Another way to say it is, guilt is localized, while shame and grief are widespread. Guilt is easier to treat than the infection itself.

The 'Guilt Offering' established in the Old Testament was established to make amends for an individual's wrongdoing. Jesus speaks of the guilt offering in the Sermon on the Mount, and says this,

> *Therefore, if you are offering your gift at the altar and there remember that your brother or sister has something against you; leave your gift there in front of the altar. First, go and be reconciled to them; then come and offer your gift.*

And He follows that with this caveat,

> *Settle matters quickly with your adversary who is taking you to court. Do it while you are still with him on the way, or your adversary may hand you over to the judge, and the judge may hand you over to the officer, and you may be thrown into prison.*

In layman's terms, Jesus is saying that if you borrowed your neighbor's John Deere X700 signature series riding lawn mower with a diesel engine and High Deep and High Capacity mower decks—GIVE IT BACK! And not only is He saying to give it back, but He is saying pay them interest for the time you kept it. And if you broke it—fix it! Return things better than you found them. Or said another way, "If I owe Smith ten dollars and God forgives me, that doesn't pay Smith."[111]

A transgression is a willful sin. It is a wound that is inflicted on another when we commit an act like robbery, baring false witness, abuse of any kind, and gossip. As humans, we can be guilty of committing transgressions against each other. The Bible says to *owe no man anything*, even if what you owe him is an apology. Go to them, set it right. My husband says, "Sorry shifts the atmosphere."[112] Guilt is a great motivator to setting things right and cleaning the slate. However, guilt can quickly spin into shame. Like Adam and

Eve, it can go from "I did something wrong" to "I am something wrong" in two shakes of a lamb's tail.

Don't underestimate the power of a genuine heart-felt apology. In other words, don't be stingy with saying "sorry," because you don't know how much that person might need to hear it and you don't know how much you might need to say it. Your "sorry" might be the difference between life and death for both them, and you, spiritually, emotionally, and yes, even physically speaking.

On the other hand, if someone has wounded you, there's a good chance they might never apologize or even acknowledge it. So, if you've been waiting to hear them say, "I'm sorry"—stop postponing! You don't need their acknowledgment or their apology to start clearing the wing jam, that is, the *injustice* jam, or the center jam, that is, the *'what about me'* jam, before you start picking off the logs to prevent a full-on log jam in your life. Forgive quickly.

Jesus was *wounded* for you. He was *bruised* for you. He made a way for you to have healing and wholeness; even without the offender acknowledging the pain or the injury they caused you. On the cross, Christ acknowledged the pain and the injury done to you. All at once, His blood reached back into the past and forward into the future. *His pain for yours.*

The mill where the logs go to be repurposed

Photo credit: West Branch Historical Preservation Committee,
http://themaineboomhouses.org/photos-from-the-pas

11

THE MILL

"Forgiveness is the fragrance a violet sheds beneath the foot that hath crushed it"

— Mark Twain

IN 1968, MY dad, who worked at the mill in Winslow was sorting logs into different pockets with his pickaroon pole—spruce with spruce, hemlock with hemlock, pine with pine, when he slipped and fell into the river. He couldn't swim and fortunately for him, another river driver was able to fish him out before he sank to the bottom or before he was swept downriver with the fast flowing current and sluiced through a dam. As strange as it sounds—a river driver who can't swim—many couldn't swim. Whether they were working on top of an icy dam feeding logs through the sluice gates or floating downriver standing on a slippery spinning log. They relied heavily upon their cork boots, balancing skills, quick footedness, and pickaroon poles to maintain steadiness,

Because the spikes on their cork boots kept them from slipping, if the spikes became caked with tree bark, leaves, and mud, they could lose their footing. It was the river driver's job to maintain clean spikes and clean soles. Those who lost their lives from being crushed between logs, hit by flying debris, fed through dams, or drowning, when their bodies washed up, if they washed up, would have their cork boots removed and nailed to a nearby tree where the body was found to mark the spot as a memorial.

Remember in chapter 6 how there were two lions mentioned, Jesus the Lion of Judah and the devil? Only one of them wore cork boots.

We forget this sometimes.

Which lion are you feeding? Are your feet shod with the preparation of the Gospel of peace or with chaos?

The lion you feed is the one that grows.

It took me six months to realize that I'd been feeding the wrong one. My soul was dirty and caked with bitterness and muddied from the injustice of it all. It was time for me to take out the wire brush and clean the spikes on my cork boots...

IN APRIL OF 2000, the sun splayed through the stain glass window like fingers on God's outstretched hand reaching for me. The small of my back pressed into the hard pew.

That night, Rita and Wayne were late to the service; the only seats left were the ones in front of me. As the worship leader sang, I stared at Rita's raven colored hair draped over the back of the pew and waited for the right moment to do what God was prodding me to do. The drummer drummed loudly, and the saints stood clapping and swaying, and before I could talk myself out of it, I leaned forward and tapped her on the shoulder. Rita's head rotated around and with a sharp piercing glance, she flicked her hair with her fingertips as she turned back around to face the pulpit.

Knowing she never admitted to robbing my house, I knew I was taking a risk, but I trusted the still small voice that told me to forgive. Trusting my gut, I leaned forward and tapped her again.

Her head rotated around and this time she mouthed, "Wh—at?"

And before she could turn back around, I quickly motioned for her to come sit with me.

She rolled her eyes and sighed, but then stood.

I took a deep breath and watched as she made her way to me and sank down beside me.

"What do you want?" she said with downcast eyes.

"I want to tell you something…" I said with a pause.

She tilted her head, her brow made a question mark, and she peered up at me over her wire frames as if to ask, *What is it?*

Without warning, I threw my arms around her, pulled her close in a warm embrace, and with tears streaming down my face, I whispered in her ear the nine words God gave me. "I forgive you! I release you of your burden."

Rita broke like a communion wafer and began sobbing in my arms and in deep broken breaths, she cried, "I don't understand. Why would you forgive me? I'm the one who did you wrong."

I could taste the salt at the back of my throat. "It's okay," I said as tears ran down my face. "I forgive you!"

Right there in the middle of song service, the log jam broke and for the first time since Halloween we stood and worshipped together and sang.

I lifted my hands toward heaven and looked up as I sang. A strange barely visible shadow floated upward from where I stood, like the black smoke from an untrimmed wick, and when it reached the ceiling, it disappeared leaving me with an overwhelming sense of peace and joy and love.

I was free (an excerpt from my memoir coming soon, titled *In the Land of Canaan: A Little Girl's Giants*). [114]

In that moment, I realized two things: There is a real spirit of unforgiveness that attaches itself when you harbor bitterness and resentment and injustice, and I never want to be attached to it again.

FORGIVENESS HAS A SCENT

One of my most favorite smells in the world is the smell of sweat and saw dust on my husband. I love when he is working with wood and the yellow shavings blow through the air hole on the skill saw and clings to the sweat. There's something about the smell of the saw dust that says something new is on its way. Something new is happening. Something new is in the works. And as a river driver there is nothing better than rounding the bend, catching the scent of freshly cut wood shavings wafting through the air, seeing the mill on the hill, and the conveyer belt loaded with logs on their way into the mill. Then it hits you, that He makes all things new. He's about to do with your logs what He's doing with those logs and all the logs before that—repurpose for a purpose.

Remember the *tzitzit* in chapter 2, otherwise known as the tassels which hang from the four corners of the Jewish prayer shawl? The blue string, is otherwise known in Hebrew as the *Shamash*, meaning, caretaker or attendant?

Good. I didn't think you'd forget.

Here's something else you should know about the *tzitzit*. The eight strings that come together to form the tassel are called 'blossoms.'

How crazy is that?

What do blossoms and fragrance have to do with forgiveness? you ask.

Great questions! Besides the eight tassels symbolizing new beginnings, here's what… blossoms give off a pleasant aroma.

Our neighbor has a magnolia tree with blossoms the size of a human head. When it blooms, I like to pick a flower and place it in a large bowl of water on the kitchen table. The fragrance from the flower fills the house and reminds me of Mark Twain's words: "Forgiveness is the fragrance that the violet sheds on the heel that has crushed it."[115]

I don't know if Mark Twain knew it, but there is a whole science behind the sense of smell. The sense of smell is deeply connected with human emotion and memory. A powerful experience can be directly linked to the olfactory system,[116] or sense of smell, whether it is a "good smell" or a "bad smell." A sudden scent can cause a memory to rush back to mind. This can be good if you smell the scent of Avon and mint filtered cigarettes and remember your grandmother, who was nurturing, or it can be bad if you smell the scent of Avon and mint filtered cigarettes and think of your grandmother, who was not nurturing.

The Bible connects the sense of smell with the human experience as well. We first hear about the hyssop branch in Exodus 12, when Moses tells the people to take hyssop and dip it in lambs' blood and strike the top and sides of the doorpost on the houses.

Why hyssop?

Hyssop is a mint smelling herb that grows on three-foot stalks with beautiful flowers. The hyssop branch releases its fragrance when struck against something. Here it was the doorposts and lintels.

Notice how the mint fragrance isn't released until the branch is struck. Pain and suffering are often the tools God uses to crack open the Alabaster box within us.

In the Gospel of John, we see the hyssop branch mentioned again. This time the hyssop branch is used to raise a sponge filled with vinegar to the lips of Jesus. The Jewish audience would have immediately made the connection between the hyssop branch the soldiers used and the hyssop branch Moses wrote about the night the death angel passed over the houses where the blood had been applied.

But that's not all!

Let's dive deeper into the Day of Atonement and look at another unique aspect, one that has to do with smell. There are five things that the Jewish people refrain from doing on the Day of Atonement. They are:

1. No food for 25 hours
2. No leather shoes
3. No bathing or washing
4. No makeup, perfume, or lotions
5. No marital relations

Rabbi Mordecai Griffen explains that these prohibitions have to do with the human senses and links them with the creation account. In the garden, Eve *saw* the fruit, she *took* the fruit, she *ate* the fruit, and Adam and Eve *heard* the voice of the LORD God walking in the cool of the day.[117]

The only sense not mentioned in the Adam and Eve story is *smell*. According to Jewish tradition, the sense of smell remains a spiritual pleasure on the Day of Atonement (Talmud, Berachot 43b) and for this reason, the sages teach that when the Messiah returns, he is going to judge the people by their smell. They get this from Isaiah 11:3. Ellicot's Commentary for English Readers notes "Some commentators, however, interpret *he shall find a sweet savour* to mean, 'scent' or 'smell,' either as the organ or the object of perception."[118]

Rabbi Mordecai Griffen says that "although the Jewish people refrain on this day from bathing, washing, putting on makeup, lotion, cologne, or perfume, they are encouraged to smell pleasant fragrances."[119]

Jewish literature teaches that during the time of offering incense the priest attending to the altar of incense would pray and intercede on behalf of the people. The incense would be offered twice a day, once in the morning and once in the evening. The golden altar of incense had a ram's horn on each of the four corners with which the high priest would dab each horn with blood on the Day of Atonement.

The incense was a sweet-smelling fragrance that wafted up to heaven and filled the nostrils of God. It wafted out into the streets signifying to the people that it was the time of offering incense. According to the Gospel of Luke, it was customary for the people to pray at the time of incense as well. Just as the high priest would pray for the people as he offered incense, the book of Hebrews tells us that Christ our Great High Priest prays and intercedes on our behalf.

Jesus is all in all!—

Not only was He the Sacrifice and the Sacrificer, but He was also the One who offered incense and was pleased by it.

Forgiveness is the fragrance the violet sheds beneath the foot that hath crushed it. When you forgive the difficult and unforgiveable thing it becomes a sweet-smelling fragrance in the nostrils of God. It leaves a traceable scent for others to find their way downstream to the Mill.

Cleaning the rear

Photo credit: West Branch Historical Preservation Committee,
http://themaineboomhouses.org/photos-from-the-past/

12

CLEANING THE REAR

"To be a Christian means to forgive the inexcusable because God has forgiven the inexcusable in you"

– C.S. Lewis

ONCE THE LOGS reached the mill, there was still one very important step for the river drivers to do and that was to head back up stream to retrieve all the logs left behind on embankments, hung up on boulders and trees, and stranded in the shallows and float them downriver to the mill. The river drivers only got paid for the logs that made it to the mill, therefore, *cleaning the rear*[120] as they called it, was an essential part of the job, if they wanted full payment for the logs.

Although I had forgiven Rita, there was still one very important step left in the process, to forgive my uncle. I hadn't seen or spoken to him in fourteen years; Yet, I felt strongly that the same words I spoke to Rita, I needed to speak to him. Due to the sensitive nature, I wasn't sure how to reach him or who to call to get his contact information without sounding the alarm or making the extended family think the 'trouble-maker with a capital 'T'' had reemerged.

The *how* came a few months later, when the phone rang, and I knew it was now or never. The time had come to reach back into the past and retrieve all the stray and stranded logs and float them downstream to the Mill. The phone call that changed my life went like this…

IT'S MOM. I can tell by her cough. I hear the flick of the Bic and wonder what number she's on for the day. She smokes and not in a charming Hollywood kind of way, but more like a guppy sucking air way. First the unfiltered, then the filtered before switching to the Lite, and the phlegmy cough—not the cigarettes fault. *Never is*. Allergies or pollen or something like that.

Mom clears her throat. "Hope you're sitting down." Her words coupled with her thick Maine accent send shivers up my spine and into my hair.

My heart pounds. *Is Dad all right?*

"Your uncle's had a massive heart attack and the doctors don't expect him to make it. Serves him right. Hope he dies. He'd be doing us all a favor then."

Uncle Jerry?

Memories flood my head and my heart. Unpleasant memories. Memories of pain and rejection. But something surges past the memories. Regret. "He can't die! I haven't told him I forgive him yet—"

A series of loud hisses snake through the phone from Mom's lips to my ears. "That man's a monster! I thought you'd be happy! Your sisters sure were. Why Pauline said, 'she'd go to his funeral just to spit on his grave'."

Mom's answer doesn't surprise me. A lot of people would tell me that my uncle did the unforgivable. Yet, my eyes well. Without answering her, I ask, "Do you know which hospital?"

Mom talks fast and angry. "After all he did to you girls. After all he put our family through. You're gonna forgive him? He's never so much as said he was sorry. You're a fool Francine…a fool."

"I forgave him a long time ago, but I need to tell him."

"Go ahead…Call him! He's at the Portland hospital. Do what you want, but don't say, I didn't tell you so."

The call ends, and a lump invades my throat. I think of the other guys who took what wasn't theirs and Aunt Mable, who was pure evil. I might not be able to make it right with them right now, but this, this thing I could.

Before talking myself out of it, I force my fingers to dial 4-1-1. The silence stretches, and I wait for the operator to connect me.

My hands tremble without permission and butterflies freestyle in my stomach. Voices. So many voices entangle my thoughts. *Should I be doing this? What if he doesn't recall or better yet, what if he denies it all?*

I listen for him to say 'hello' and gaze out the kitchen window at my three boys, Myles, Seth, and Ethan, playing baseball with their dad and tagging bases marked with shoes. I smile at how fortunate I am, and find myself remembering, and welling up. I remember when I was eleven and the doctor saying, "The damage is too great. I don't know if she can have children." I remember Mom crying.

I remember in detail, the little brown house with the mustard-trimmed door, tucked between Grandma Dodge's farmhouse and Aunt Mable's trailer in Canaan, Maine. The backsides of our properties fenced in by Grandpa's junkyard with a thin stretch of pines separating the garbled metal from our view, and cornfields bordering both sides; one to the left of Grandma's house and the other, to the right of Mable's.

But now I'm back. My hands shake, and I press the receiver against my ear and stare out the kitchen window.

"Hello," a weak and gravelly voice says.

It's him!

A sinking feeling comes over me as I remember the two dimes and a nickel he always gave me, the Mafia-styled car, the six-legged octopus, the green school bus, and the spring of '87, when warm chocolate chip cookies exchanged hands; I was thirteen.

The sound of his voice makes me feel small like it's me *David*, and him, *Goliath,* again. Fear pumps through my veins like it did when I was small, and I push the button to end the call.

Despite the sweaty palms and knot in my throat, I summon the courage to dial him back, and when I hear his voice the second time, I breathe deep and say in one breath, "This is Francine! Please don't hang up." I pause and listen. No dial tone. So, I keep going. "I forgive you! I release you of your burden."

Once the words are out, I feel my heart thud against my chest. These are the words I've wanted to say for some time. These are the words that I needed to say to set me free.

I press the phone against my ear and wait for a dial tone. When there is none, I quickly say, "We both know it hasn't done your heart any good carrying this burden around. Do you know what burden I'm referring to?"

There's a long pause, and I add, "I know you're not alone, because I can hear others in your room, so if 'ayuh' is the only answer you can give, then 'ayuh' is fine with me."

His breathing is labored, and I count in my head one Mississippi, two Mississippi, three Mississippi, four Mississippi, before he responds with "Ayuh."

I squeeze the receiver in my hand and push back the urge to weep out loud. "I know the doctors don't expect you to make it through the night, so I want you to know I'm praying for you."

"Thanks, I need all the prayer I can get right now."

I gaze at the plush green fern growing on the porch and am drawn back to the relentless winters in Maine, where the true sign of spring was not a day marked on the calendar, but by the emerald-green fiddlehead. All ferns start with the fiddlehead. The fiddlehead is a fern, before it unfolds.

"Goodbye," I say as I pick up the pen and begin to write, glad that this season of my life has finally drawn to a close.[121] (Excerpt from my second memoir soon to be published: *Fiddleheads*.)

Using wooden boats to clear a jam and to steer the logs downstream

Photo credit: West Branch Historical Preservation Committee,
http://themaineboomhouses.org/photos-from-the-past/

13

BOATS, ROPES & HOPE

"Forgiveness is giving up the hope that the past could have been any different"
— Oprah Winfrey

THE RIVER DRIVERS couldn't have worked the river without the oarsmen who navigated the flat-bottomed wooden boats down the river as they stood up pushing and steering the logs downstream with their pickaroon poles. If, while floating the logs downstream, they became snagged by an island or a boulder in the rapids, then a line would be attached to both sides of the boat and anchored to both shores. The boat would then be carefully lowered down to the center jam, so the logs could be cleared.[122]

What does a line and a boat have to do with forgiveness? you ask.

The answer is—
Everything!

Forgiveness is the bloodline of *Hope*.

It's in our spiritual DNA to forgive and when we choose not to forgive, we go against the very nature of God, and turn against the *Hope* that things can be different.

Hope is assurance in something not yet seen. It's the anticipation behind every word of Eve, when she bare Cain, and said, "I have gotten a man from the LORD." As if to say, *Is this the One who will crush the head of the snake?*

Do you remember how the *tzitzit* or tassel or blossom, whichever you prefer to call it, is made by running three white strings and one blue string through a hole and looping them over to make eight strings, and how the blue string wraps around all the other strings to make one cord? Well, the blue string in the *tzitzit* or tassel or blossom is a tangible reminder of hope.

What do you mean? you ask.

Here, let me explain.

One of the words for hope in the Hebrew is the word *tikvah*, which means, "cord, measuring line, expectation, and outcome. It is the act of combining multiple strands and coiling those into a single, much stronger cable."[123]

From the start of the logging season, the river drivers had confidence in something not yet seen, and they did whatever was necessary to obtain *that* outcome. Although they couldn't see the mill, they *saw* it, and trusted the process, the same way Abraham saw his promise and trusted the process when he left home to look for the city with foundations whose builder and maker was God.

One thing is for sure, as a river driver, you have to *see* the mill, before you can *ever* get the logs there.

Hope is a collection of moments that when combined becomes the way in, the way out, and the way through.
A line.
A cord.
A rope.
Amazing, huh?

There's a story in the book of Joshua that I love about a red cord. It says that Joshua sent spies to the city of Jericho to spy it out, and while there, they lodged at the house of a harlot named Rahab. When the king of Jericho got wind that Rahab harbored spies, he commanded her to turn them over. Instead, she hid them on the rooftop, told the king that they had left, and that she didn't know which way they had gone.

After sparing the lives of the spies, Rahab made a request. Rahab knew in her heart that the LORD had already given the land of Jericho to the children of Israel. She had hope. That her life and her family's lives would be spared from destruction when the army of Israel returned to take Jericho. The spies agreed to her request and told her to mark her house by hanging a red cord out of the window.

A red cord.

Why is this important? you ask.

Like forgiveness, hope is forward moving. So, if you're hoping for the past to be any different, then you're hoping in the wrong direction. Hope in reverse is despair. It takes forward-moving-hope to *see* what God can do with your painful experiences.

Rahab's red cord was a *tikvah*.
The scapegoat's scarlet cord was a *tikvah*.
The blue string in the tassel was and is a *tikvah*.

Although Rahab hadn't yet been delivered, she eagerly awaited the day she would be. *The red cord was her way out.*

Rahab's story about a cord and a wall makes me think of another story about a cord and a wall in the book of Zechariah. This time the cord was used as a measuring line to measure the walls of Jerusalem. This is an interesting story, because here we have two angels. The first angel tells the second angel to run and tell Zechariah that Jerusalem will be a city without walls.

Did you catch that?

According to the definition of hope, the measuring line was also a *tikvah.*

Here's something else...in the Hebrew, the word *Jerusalem* means, "City of peace."

The angelic announcement was really an announcement of *unlimited peace.* Which is what you get when you forgive. *Shalom.* Lewis B. Smedes said, "To forgive is to set a prisoner free and discover that the prisoner was you."[124] If you want peace, you need to forgive. That doesn't mean forgetting what happened or excusing it. It's freeing up the river, so that peace can flow to you and through you.

Isaiah writes about hope when he writes about a barren woman and a cord. Here's what he says,
*Sing, O barren, thou that didst not bear; break forth into singing, and cry aloud, thou that didst not travail with child: for more are the children of the desolate than the children of the married wife, saith the LORD. Enlarge the place of thy tent, and let them stretch forth the curtains of thine habitations: spare not, **lengthen thy cords**, and strengthen thy stakes;*

Isaiah tells the barren woman to expand the canopy of her tent, to lengthen the cords of her tent, and to strengthen the stakes of her tent, because she is going to have children. Lots of them.

When I picture the barren woman singing, crying, and preparing her tent, I picture a bunch of River Jacks and River Jills singing and shouting as they steered, persevered, moved, pushed, and blasted their way downstream with thousands of tons of logs, point to point, logging camp to logging camp, boom to boom with a grueling grit, because they had confidence that there was a mill. *Though they couldn't see it, they could see it!*

You can see how groundbreaking this is—from the lines on the boat to the blue string in the *tzitzit* to Rahab's red cord to the scapegoat's scarlet cord to the measuring line to the barren woman lengthening the cords of her tent—they all had one thing in common and that was relentless hope. Or in river driver language, grueling grit.

I love what Paul says,
But this one thing I do, forgetting those things which are behind, and reaching forth unto those things which are before.

Paul was talking about hope. A collection of small moments that when coiled together is forward-moving. The collection is *progress*. The outcome is *purpose*. To prove this, the Gospel of Matthew lists Rahab, the Harlot, in Jesus' family tree.

What?!

I'm serious! A harlot.

See for yourselves…
This is the genealogy of Jesus the Messiah the son of David, the son of Abraham:
Abraham was the father of Isaac,

Isaac the father of Jacob,
Jacob the father of Judah and his brothers,
Judah the father of Perez and Zerah, whose
Mother was Tamar,
Perez the father of Hezron,
Hezron the father of Ram,
Rm the father of Nahshon,
Nahshon the father of Salmon,
Salmon the father of Boaz, whose mother was
Rahab...[125]

How cool is that?

Paul wasn't saying leave all the mixed memories behind and forget the negative experiences. He understood that the direction the eyes looked was the direction in which the heart went. Your heart follows your eyes.

Hope is forward moving. Despair is anything else.

In the Bible there are examples of what happens when we put our *hand to the plow*, so to speak, and then look back. One such example would be when Israel left Egypt. In the book of Acts, the writer wanted the reader to know that Israel returned to bondage in their hearts. It was their negative outlook and constant complaining that caused the eleven-day journey to last forty years. A second example would be when Lot and his family escaped from Sodom and Gomorrah. His wife looked back and became a pillar of salt. A third example would be when the prophet of Judah left the presence of King Jeroboam. After being warned, he went back the *same* way he came, and a lion met him in the way and devoured him...

Like the prophet, which way you go determines which lion you choose—*Peace or Chaos.*

So, if you're looking for an apology, hoping the offender will acknowledge the pain, still waiting for the 'why' behind the *what,* or wishing the past could be any different, then you're hoping in the wrong direction. Or as Jesus would say, "You're kicking against the pricks."

What does that mean? you ask.

These words Jesus spoke to Saul of Tarsus, who became Paul the Apostle while he was on his way to Damascus. The prick has to do with an ox goad which is a long stick with a sharp hook on the end that a farmer uses to steer the oxen when plowing the field.[126] It's a tool used to get the oxen to change directions. If the ox kicked against the sharp tip, then it would stick into its flesh. The harder the ox kicked the deeper the goad went.

Holding a grudge is *you* kicking against the pricks. *It's you hurting yourself!*

Forgiveness is counterintuitive. That means, the best way to get even is to forgive.

The scripture says that when you forgive your enemy, you heap coals of fire on their head. That means when you treat your enemy with kindness and do good to them, you melt their hard-heart with God's love and in the process, you melt yours.

Job said,
But he knoweth the way that I take: when he hath tried me, I shall come forth as gold.

How apropos. The river driver who lost his children, possessions, health, and wealth all in the same day, said, "I shall come forth as gold."

Forgiveness is *you* hoping in the right direction. It's the day-after-dayness of moving the logs from point to point, logging camp to logging camp, boom to boom, whether you feel like it or not—knowing that you can't change what happened but having the confidence that God will make something lasting of the *logs* at the Mill. It's the daily grind of steering and pushing the offenses, real or perceived, downstream until one day you wake up and realize that you have no more bitterness and resentment toward that person who mistreated you, stole from you, harmed you.

God will take your logs and make them your legacy. But you have to get them to the Mill first.

In the same way that hope is a collection of small moments…forgiveness is a process. Suffering becomes experience; experience becomes hope; hope becomes the way out—not just for you, but for all those who are where you once were.

All logs have value at the Mill where payment is made and repurposing takes place. Otherwise, what do we do with all the bitterness, resentment, and injustice?

If your logs never reach the Mill, you've wasted your suffering.

God wants all your logs, big and small!

The Mill is the goal. In order to move the collection of hurts, traumas, and negative experiences from 'the mouth of shame' to 'the mouth of God,' you have to stop looking back and start looking forward. As a river driver, you have to see the end from the beginning, even when the two spectrums *seem* like a hundred miles apart and even when it *feels* impossible.

Lillian Disney and a reporter were discussing the magnitude of Disneyland at the theme park's grand opening. The reporter said,

"It's too bad Walt couldn't be here to see it." She replied, "Oh, Walt saw it, or you wouldn't be here."[127]

Hope is about vision. It's the heart-map that guides you to completion.

Paul writes in Romans,
For we are saved by hope: but hope that is seen is not hope: for what a man seeth, why doth he yet hope for? But if we hope for that we see not, then do we with patience wait for it.

What Paul is saying is that you have to see it with your spiritual eyes, before you can see it with your natural eyes.

Rahab saw deliverance.

Zechariah saw unlimited peace.

The barren woman saw a tent full of children.

Abraham saw the promised land.

Walt Disney saw a theme park.

The river drivers saw the mill.

Jesus saw the cross.

What do you see?

James E. Faust quoted Dr. Sidney Simon, saying, "Forgiveness is freeing up and putting to better use the energy once consumed by holding grudges, harboring resentment, and nursing unhealed wounds. It is rediscovering the strength we always had and relocating our limitless compacity to understand and accept other people and ourselves."[128]

The good news is that no matter what juncture of the river you're at—you can finish—you can get the logs to the Mill. *How do I know?* Because God has surrounded you with a great company of river drivers, others who have gone on before you and have dog-eared, stamped, and filed away their stories on the pages of time. And now they line the heavenly banks singing and shouting and cheering you on...
Job,
Joseph,
Corrie Ten Boom,
Dr. Martin Luther King Jr.
Maya Angelou.
The list goes on.

When God looks at you, He sees a completed work. *He sees what your logs have become. Not what they could be.*

How do I know?

Because Paul tells us.

When does he do this? When he writes to the church at Rome, saying,
God calls those things which be not as though they were.

And this to the church at Colossae,
Ye are complete in Him.

Gideon was called a Mighty Man of Valor before he did the courageous thing that he was called to. Abraham was called a 'father of many nations' twenty-five years before having his son Isaac.

As a river driver, the daily process of picking up your pickaroon pole and moving the logs a little further downstream each day is you moving toward your ultimate purpose for which you were created.

I can almost smell the sawdust. *Can't you?*

Good.

Now keep going!

And who knows, when you finally reach the Mill, you might find yourself saying, "Maybe this is how it was meant to be the whole time."

Markings on the logs to indicate ownership

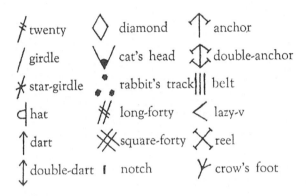

twenty

girdle

star-girdle

hat

dart

double-dart

diamond

cat's head

rabbit's track

long-forty

square-forty

notch

anchor

double-anchor

belt

lazy-v

reel

crow's foot

14

ROUGH WATERS, SMOOTH LOGS, ALL THINGS

"Before Nelson Mandela was arrested in 1962, he was an angry relatively young man, he founded the ANC's military wing. When he was released, he surprised everyone because he was talking about reconciliation and forgiveness and not about revenge"

— Desmond Tutu

YOU DON'T KNOW what you don't know. *I didn't know I wasn't supposed to be born.* That is, until Mom told me. But only after I asked her if twins ran in the family. I remember the first time I heard those words; I was twenty-three-years old, the same age she was when the doctor put her on a fertility drug called Clomid to try to correct her hormones. Somehow, the doctor failed to mention, 'No intimate relations for a two-week period after completing the medicine.' And so, when Mom returned for her check-up, she found out that she was pregnant with Charlene and me.

Mom's words make me think of David when he fought Goliath. How he wasn't supposed to be *there,* like I wasn't supposed to be *here.* He was a boy. His father Jesse sent him to the Jewish encampment with food for his brothers who were soldiers in Saul's army.

Which brings me to this. People have long been captivated by the story of the shepherd boy, who slayed the giant with a sling and a stone. In 1501, Michelangelo, began sculpting a giant statue of *David* from a massive hunk of marble. It took three years of chipping away at the marble with a chisel and a hammer, before his vision of *David* would fully emerge.[129] When asked how he created such a masterpiece, Michelangelo replied, "His David was in the stone clamoring to be freed."[130]

Did you catch that?

Michelangelo's *David* was in there the whole time. All Michelangelo had to do was remove the parts that didn't fit his vision.

This is us.

Pain and suffering are God's chisel and hammer, and over time, God removes the parts of us that don't fit His vision.

God is the Sculptor. The masterpiece He is chiseling is you!

Michelangelo's *David* reminds me of the bark on the logs at the start of the logging season. Logs pass downstream and the force of the water washing over them and the friction of bobbing and bucking logs chips away at the thick-protective layer of bark. By the time the logs reach the mill they are mostly smooth, and all the rough parts have been stripped away and scattered along the rivers bottom.

Again, this is us.

Paul writes,
For the scripture saith unto Pharaoh, Even for this same purpose have I raised thee up, that I might shew my power in thee, and that my name might be declared throughout all the earth.

You might be thinking, *God raised up Pharaoh?*

Yup. That's what Paul said.

It's hard to imagine a loving God who would allow pain and suffering, isn't it? A God who would create such a thing as a tree of the knowledge of good and evil or raise up a Pharaoh to afflict a group of people and keep them in bondage 430 years.

On the Julian calendar 430 years equates to…

5,160 months.

107 leap years.

1,720 season changes.

22,360 weeks.

156,950 days.

525,600,430 minutes.

13,569,768,000 seconds.

Now imagine this is you.

Mixing mortar,

making bricks,

building bridges,

laying infrastructures,

paving roadways,

and building treasure cities for a group of people that look down their noses at you. (Maybe you don't have to imagine.)

And yet, Moses writes,
But the more they [Egypt] afflicted them, the more they [Israel] multiplied and grew…

By Exodus 33, we find a frustrated Moses pitched outside the camp of Israel in a tent, pleading with God to show him His glory.

Moses wanted to see more of God.

To which God said,
I will make all my goodness pass before thee, and I will proclaim the name of the Lord before thee…thou canst not see my face: for there shall no man see me, and live. And the Lord said, Behold, there is a place by me, and thou shalt stand upon a rock: and it shall come to pass, while my glory passeth by, that I will put thee in a cleft of the rock, and will cover thee with my hand while I pass by: and I will take away mine hand, and thou shalt see my back parts; but my face shall not be seen.

To which I want to know, what more could Moses have possibly wanted to see?

It's a real question, for real people, in real times. Moses had already seen…

A talking burning bush.

Water turned to blood.

Frogs.

Lice.

Flies.

Boils.

Cattle die.

Hail.

Locusts.

Darkness.

Egypt's firstborn die.

A cloud protecting them by day.

A pillar of fire protecting them by night.

Red Sea part.

Pharaoh's army drowned.

Bitter waters made sweet.

Manna from heaven.

A leprous hand healed.

Quails galore.

A giant finger chiseling tables of stone.

Water from a rock.

The list goes on.

Moses' story is unique. He's the adopted grandson of Pharaoh turned rogue shepherd-leader. Though, I must admit the first time I read his story in its entirety, I shook my mental finger at God and wanted a do-over, a rewrite, a Hollywood alternate ending with all the bells and whistles.

Moses spent 40 years in Egypt as Pharaoh's grandson, 40 years in Midian shepherding his father-in-law's sheep, 40 years wandering in circles in a desert with 600,000 newly freed people,
to
never
step
foot
in
the
Promised
Land.

Wait!—What?!

My thoughts exactly!

God takes him up to mount Nebo, the highest point in Moab and allows him to see the land the children of Israel will possess. And after giving Moses a good look, says, "By the way, you ain't gonna step foot in the Promised Land! You're gonna die right here in this mount. I want Joshua to take them the rest of the way." (My words, not Gods')

That's not fair! Moses traded the possibility of becoming the next in line to the throne. He gave up the comfort and wealth of Egypt to wander in the wilderness...and for what? you say.

Deep breath. (Now put your mental finger away.)

It's easy to get caught up in the injustice of it all. *What we think should have happened.* I understand Moses disobeyed God when he struck the rock twice, but I might have done the same if I were in his sandals. Every time an obstacle arose, the people blamed Moses for bringing them into the wilderness to die and wanted to overthrow him as their leader.

This makes me think of the logs on the log drive. Multiple logging companies used the Kennebec River to float their logs to the mill. Which meant each log had to be stamped with a series of axe marks to create a symbol to indicate ownership so that they could be sorted at the mill by company for payout purposes.[131]

The next thought may sound as random as the last paragraph but stick with me, I'll circle back and string it all together. I promise—

I love how the writer of the Gospel of John includes such details as two angels sitting in the empty tomb where Jesus' body once lay, one at the head and one at the feet.

Still there?

Good.

Since the New Testament hadn't been written and compiled yet, the Gospel of John intentionally uses breadcrumbs to draw us back to the Old Testament, back to the tabernacle in the wilderness to the Ark of the Covenant with the two angels sitting on the Mercy Seat facing each other. He uses even more breadcrumbs to draw us back to the two angels in the garden protecting the way of the Tree of Life, in order to retell it through the lens of Christ.

Hmm.

But the writer of the gospel doesn't stop there. He includes other details, like the bit about Jesus telling Thomas to feel the nail scars with his fingers and thrust his hand into his side on the *eighth* day after His resurrection. Which leads me to wonder why Thomas was able to touch Him, when just a few days earlier Mary Magdalene wasn't allowed to touch His resurrected body. John intentionally mentions...

two angels,
the eighth day,
and don't touch.

All details we should be asking ourselves: what are they here for?

You already know *eight* symbolizes 'new beginnings' in the Hebrew. But did you know that when Aaron, the high priest was consecrated for the work of the LORD in the Tabernacle in the Wilderness, no one was allowed to touch Him until the *eighth* day?

Not to mention, the Levites used eight poles to carry the sacred furniture belonging to the tabernacle in the wilderness: Ark of the Covenant, Brazen Altar, Table of Shewbread, and Altar of Incense.

Hmm, again.

The Gospel of John differs from the other gospels. John looks at Jesus from the inside, while Matthew, Mark, and Luke look at Him from the outside. John makes a point to capture such details as Jesus calling Himself the *I Am*—the Old Testament name by which God revealed Himself to Moses in the burning bush. Not to mention, in his gospel, John captures *eight* specific *I Am* statements made by Jesus—

I Am the Bread of Life
I Am the Light of the World
I Am the Door
I Am the Good Shepherd
I Am the Resurrection and the Life
I Am the Way and the Truth and the Life
I Am the Vine
Before Abraham was I Am.

Now, let's talk about the burning bush and the ancient Covenant name *I Am*...

Jewish tradition and many scholars believe that the burning bush was a burning *thorn* bush. During Moses day, and still today, there is nothing uncommon about a burning bush in the desert. Naturally, when we picture a desert, we picture—scorching heat—no rain—dry shrubs—animal carcasses—tumble weeds—sand—sand dunes—and sandstorms. So, you see what I mean, when I say there is nothing uncommon about a burning thorn bush in a desert full of dry thorn bushes, unless of course, the bush that is burning isn't consumed, and then you stop to wonder, marvel, and draw near.

Yet, of all the forms God could have taken on to appear to Moses in, He chose a burning thorn bush. We'll get back to that part momentarily, but before we do, there's something else you should know. The appearance of God to man is called a *theophany*.[132] It's when the invisible God is made visible by taking on a form to communicate with His created beings. An example of this is in Genesis 18. God took on the form of an angel and appeared to Abraham and Sarah to communicate the important message that they were going to have a son.

The Jews have always believed in One God, and that this One God could be seen inserting Himself into His own creation and becoming a part of it through theophanies, like the cloud by day, the pillar of fire by night, the angel that wrestled with Jacob, the angel in the burning thorn bush, and the smoking fire pot.

Here's a question:
Why do you think theophanies ceased at Bethlehem?

And why do you think God chose a burning thorn bush to reveal Himself to Moses in?

The thorns represent pain and suffering. Not only the pain and suffering of the children of Israel in Egypt, but the pain and suffering the Messiah would endure during the last hours of His life...

Log #1:
They pressed a crown of thorns into His head.

Log #2:
They put a purple robe on Him and mocked Him.

Log #3:
They smote Him with their hands.

Log #4:
His own people rejected Him.

Log #5:
He was whipped thirty-nine times.

Log#6:
He was forced to carry His own cross

Log #7:
Soldiers stripped Him naked and gambled for His clothes.

Log #8:
A soldier gave Him vinegar on a sponge to drink.

Log #9:
A soldier pierced His side with a sword.

Log #10:
He was spat upon.

See what I mean?

Although the physical body of Jesus wasn't back there in the burning bush, the Eternal Spirit that indwelt Christ was. The Gospel of John paints the portrait of Jesus being all in all. Brush stroke upon brush stroke, he reveals to the Jewish people that the God whom they seek is tented among them in flesh and blood. In chapter 2 of John's Gospel, he captures these tell-all words of Jesus,

Destroy this temple and in three days, I will raise it up.

To which, John adds these words,
But he spake of the temple of his body.

I love that part—

There's something else going on just below the surface. John wants us to see that Jesus is the bodily temple that houses the glory and presence of God. And even more so, Jesus is all of the furnishings of the temple too. Rather than show us the panoramic view like the other gospels, John zooms in to show us an up-close and personal view of Christ. John wants us to see that—

Jesus is the Candlestick.

Jesus is the Shew Bread.

Jesus is the Altar of Incense.

Jesus is the Living Water.

Jesus is the Mercy Seat.

Jesus is the Great High Priest.

Jesus is the sacrificial Lamb.

Jesus is the Scapegoat.

Jesus is the Veil.

Jesus is the Blue String.

The tabernacle in the wilderness was a type and shadow of Christ. And when Moses struck the rock twice, God became angry with him, because Christ should only suffer once. And as punishment, Moses wasn't allowed to enter the Promised Land, even though he gave up the pleasures of Egypt to suffer with the children of Israel.

Which brings me back to the question: what did Moses actually see, when he asked God to show him His glory?

Well, let's *string* it together and see…

When God said thou canst not see my face, He wasn't speaking of a literal body part. The term 'face' describes how vast and broad the Spirit of God is. God fills all-in-all and is everywhere present. Thus,

God didn't have a literal face until He came in the body of His Son, and why *theophanies* ceased at Bethlehem.

Face is used to represent the beginning, otherwise known as the creation account. Thus, God shielded Moses in the cleft of *the rock*, while His unconcealed glory passed by, so that he wouldn't be consumed by the sheer brilliance of His presence. After which, God allowed Moses to see His back parts, otherwise known as the ending, or what would come later—fifteen hundred years later. The bodily temple that would house His glory.

In the Old Testament, Moses built a tabernacle made of badger skins, so that God could be tented among His people. In the New Testament, God made the tabernacle of flesh, so that He could be tented among His people. The first was made with hands, the second without.

So, what did Moses see?

The New Testament gives us the answer. In Matthew 17, Jesus takes Peter, James, and John up into a high mountain where He is transfigured, and Matthew later writes,

And his face did shine as the sun, and his raiment was white as the light. And, behold, there appeared unto them Moses and Elias talking with him.

Moses may not have entered the Promised Land, but he saw the better part—the Promised One! He saw the glory of God in the face of Jesus Christ.

What I thought needed a re-do or a Hollywood alternate ending had the ultimate ending!

I said all that to say,

Stop wishing for an alternate ending for your story.

Victor E. Frankl, author of the book, *Man's Search for Meaning*, said, "Suffering ceases to be suffering at the moment it finds a meaning."[133]

Michelangelo's statue of *David* didn't portray the victorious David that defeated the giant, but the shepherd boy David who kept his father's sheep on the backside of a desert. The giant David faced as a youth wasn't his giant—it was Israel's giant. Just like the giant I faced in my youth wasn't my giant—it was and is the giant of all those who suffer the like afflictions of sexual abuse, rape, poverty, and injustice.

For I reckon that the sufferings of this present time are not worthy to be compared with the glory which shall be revealed in us.

Paul wrote that, and this,

*With all wisdom and understanding, he [God] made known to us the mystery of his will according to his good pleasure, which he purposed in Christ, to be put into effect when the times reach their fulfillment—to bring unity to **all things** in heaven and on earth under Christ.*

In the book, *What is the Bible?* Rob Bell shares that the phrase 'all things' comes from the Greek word *pas*, which means,
to reconcile,
to recapitulate,
to retell,
to sum up.[134]

It's a math term. It's what an accountant does. An accountant sums up numbers and reconciles books. The two books being reconciled are the Old and the New Testaments, and God does this through the Mediator, the man, Christ Jesus.

God doesn't want an alternate ending for your story. Like Moses, He wants to retell it in a new light. Here's an example. My childhood wasn't easy. You already know that...

A poor girl from Maine,
who went to the bathroom on 5-gallon buckets,
who drew water from a rusty brown handpump in the side yard,
who was sexually abused,
who was sold to men,
who was rejected by her extended family,
who was raped by a stranger in the woods.
All before the age of twelve.

All details my twelve-year-old self never would have shared with the person sitting next to me at the lunch table in junior high. *Hi! I'm Francine. I go to the bathroom on buckets...will you be my friend?* See what I mean!

But now as I retell my story and write this book, I don't leave out the shameful experiences. My difficult start has become the hope that people can grab hold of and cling to. God has repurposed the trauma of my past and made it His treasure. The painful parts of my past have become the best parts of my story.[135]

A
girl
on
the
front
row
in
a
low

chair,
as
though
she
was
sitting
Shiva.

Her brown hair covered her hands that covered her face that hid her grief. I sat Shiva with her, and in solidarity whispered, "Me too! I was raped."

See what happened there? God wants to retell your story.

This can be you! He wants to take your logs and make them your legacy. In a meaningful way.

Paul writes,
*And we know that **all things** work together for **good** to them that love God, to them who are the called according to his purpose.*

The idea that, when your mostly smooth logs reach the Mill, God will repurpose them for a purpose—the purpose which He placed in you before the worlds were framed, before He formed you in the womb, before you knew you weren't supposed to be born, before the drugs, before the alcohol, before the abortion, before the rape, before the divorce, before the loss, before the accident, before the robbery, before doing that thing you did, before the pain and the suffering—is huge!

Christ died to bring unity to all things external and internal.

Which brings me back to the logs on the log drive and the axe marks stamped on the end of each log to indicate ownership. I can't help but think of the verse where God tells the prophet Jeremiah, *I will make this people wood.*

Logs on the river drive have identifying marks. And we have wounds and scars.

The logs are us. We are the sum total of our hurts and pains. Which is why we need a Reconciler and why God was hid in Christ. To reconcile all things back to Himself.

The Apostle Paul wrote thirteen books of the New Testament, three of which were penned from prison. He was whipped with thirty-nine lashes on five separate occasions by his own people, beaten with rods three different times, shipwrecked three times, and stoned. Yet, he writes often about reconciliation, forgiveness, and the power of suffering.

Paul understood that,
suffering is the blue string that unites us.

And that,
suffering brings the Holy down to sit *shiva* with us.

Which brings me to this culmination of thought. In Acts 14, we read how Paul was stoned and left for dead outside the city gates in Lystra. But he doesn't die. Instead, he gets up and goes on to preach in Derbe, and after preaching there, he returns with wounds-and-all to Lystra, to the place where he was *just* stoned and left for dead to preach faith and to further the gospel. Paul owned his scars and wore them as a Badge of Honor, a Purple Heart of sorts, so others might see and believe.

Like forgiveness, faith is also counterintuitive. It doesn't make sense that Paul would return to the place where he was wounded.

And so, like Paul, I own my scars and wear them as a Badge of Honor, and I return in my retelling to the places where I was once wounded, so that others might see and believe that the worst parts of their story can become the best parts of their story at the Mill.

God wants all your logs.

So just say, "Here!"

He can't *cant* miss.

The Cross is the place where the logs are converted and where the retelling takes place. Jesus wasn't wounded for Himself; He was wounded for you and for me. His suffering is the ultimate "Me, too!" The Greatest River Driver to ever live uttered three words while suspended from two logs...*It is finished!* Words that changed the past, the present, and the future for all humanity.

Now I ask you, what do a bunch of river drivers in flannel shirts and cork boots have to do with forgiveness?

The answer is—
Everything!

Don't waste your suffering. Get your logs to the Mill. Christ endured the cross knowing what would come after. *Glory follows suffering.* There's a place of completion for your logs. A place where the river drive ends, and the logs get repurposed. A place where you receive double for your shame. But you've got to get the bitterness, the hatred, and the resentment to Him first.

Bearing in mind, it's not how, it's when—when you get the logs to the Mill, then God will use them. Forgiveness is a process. But the process is more than a process. It's your offering! God wants all your logs, big or small, strayed or stranded, real or perceived.

How many logs?

All of them!

This book is about river drivers and scapegoats and log jams and two dogs and forgiveness. The Spirit is always flowing, but it isn't the rivers job to get the logs to the Mill. You've got to do the doing!

So, River Driver...

Yes, that means you!

Are you ready to move those logs?

Good.

Now, grab your pickaroon pole and peavey hook and start moving them forward.

I'll meet you at the Mill!

ATTRIBUTES OF A RIVER DRIVER

Resilient
Intentional
Vigilant
Experienced
Resourceful

Determined
Rugged
Immediate
Visual
Endurance
Reliable

SCRIPTURE REFERENCES

Introduction:

1. Philippians 4:8
2. 2 Corinthians 1:24-27
3. Philippians 3:13

Chapter 1: Goats, Dogs & River Drivers

1. Matthew 15:21-28 "The Canaanite woman"
2. 2 Samuel 4:4 "The nurse and Mephibosheth"
3. 2 Samuel 9:1-9 "David and Mephibosheth"

Chapter 2: Pickaroon Poles & Peavey Hooks

1. Numbers 15:38-40 "Tassels of the four corners of their garments"
2. John 17:22 "Oneness"
3. Genesis 8:1 "God remembered Noah"
4. 2 Peter 2:5 "Noah was the eighth person saved by water"
5. John 14:2-3
6. John 14:18
7. John 14:26
8. Ephesians 4:4
9. 2 Corinthians 3:17
10. Exodus 12 "The Egyptian Passover"
11. John 1:14
12. John 10:30
13. John 14:9
14. John 14:27
15. Ephesians 4:4-6
16. Philippians 2:5
17. Romans 12:2 (NIV)
18. Numbers 11:5 (NKJV)
19. Acts 7:39
20. Colossians 3:2
21. I Corinthians 11:23
22. Proverbs 23:7
23. I Thessalonians 5:19
24. I Thessalonians 5:21
25. Psalm 51:10

26. Luke 9:23 (paraphrased)
27. Romans 12:14
28. Matthew 5:44
29. Matthew 6:11
30. Ephesians 4:26
31. Ephesians 4:32
32. 2 Corinthians 5:18
33. Matthew 5:24 (BSB)
34. Matthew 11:28
35. Ephesians 4:3
36. Matthew 5:48
37. Hebrews 12:14
38. Romans 12:14
39. Matthew 7:1
40. Romans 8:28
41. Matthew 3:2
42. Romans 5:6
43. Luke 23:34

Chapter 3: Splash Dams & Three Jams
1. Malachi 3:1
2. John 1:23
3. Ephesians 4:26
4. Matthew 5:38
5. Isaiah 43:18-19 (NIV)
6. John 7:37-38
7. I Thessalonians 5:19
8. Isaiah 61:7 (NIV)
9. Matthew 26:39
10. Luke 23:34
11. Romans 8:28

Chapter 4: Jonah & the Log Jam
1. Jonah 2:2
2. Luke 16:22 "Abraham's Bosom"
3. I Peter 3:19
4. Jonah 2:6

5.   Acts 2:27
6.   Jonah 2:7
7.   Jonah 3:1-2
8.   Matthew 12:40 "Sign of Jonah"
9.   John 2:22
10. Matthew 16:16-17
11. 2 Kings 14:25 "Jonah is first mentioned"
12. Jonah 4:2
13. Romans 12:20
14. Ephesians 4:32
15. Matthew 5:44

Chapter 5: Ash Poles & Log Booms

Chapter 6: A Lion in Cork Boots

1.   Ephesians 6:15
2.   Romans 10:15
3.   Romans 3:15
4.   Ephesians 2:13-14
5.   Ephesians 4:26
6.   2 Corinthians 5:18
7.   Ephesians 4:1-3
8.   Matthew 5:23-24
9.   Genesis 4:3-4 "Cain and Abel"
10. Revelation 18:3 "Lamb slain from the foundation of the world"
11. Genesis 4:7 "Cain's countenance"
12. Genesis 4:7 "Chattat croucheth at the petach" (Jewish Orthodox Bible)
13. I Peter 5:8 "The devil is like a roaring lion"
14. Revelation 5:5 "Lion of the tribe of Judah"
15. Romans 5:20
16. 2 Corinthians 5:19 "God was in Christ"
17. Matthew 5:25
18. Matthew 26:39
19. Matthew 26:41
20. Luke 23:34

Chapter 7: Donkey Engines & Wannigans

1.   Matthew 21:2 "Jesus calls for a donkey"

2. Luke 19:28-40 "Triumphal entry"
3. Zechariah 9:9
4. Leviticus 23:3 "Holy convocation"
5. Exodus 12 "Egyptian Passover"
6. I Peter 1:18-19
7. I Timothy 2:6
8. John 19:28 "I thirst"
9. Matthew 6:11-12
10. Matthew 18:21
11. I Kings 8:61 "Let your heart be perfect"
12. Matthew 18:23-35 (NIV)
13. Matthew 5:23-25 (NIV)
14. Matthew 7:1-2
15. Luke 10:29 "Who is my neighbor?"
16. Mark 12: 28-31 "The first of all the commandments" & "Love they neighbor as thyself"
17. Luke 6:32-36 (NIV)
18. Colossians 3:13 (BSB)
19. Ephesians 4:32 (ESV)
20. Song of Solomon 2:15 "It's the little foxes that spoil the vine"
21. Matthew 6:14
22. Matthew 5:23, 48
23. John 6:48, 51
24. I Corinthians 11:24
25. Isaiah 61:7 "double for your shame" or "For your shame ye shall have double"

Chapter 8: The Scapegoat & the River Driver
1. Isaiah 1:18 "Though your sins be as scarlet, they shall be white as snow"
2. Hebrews 10:4 "Blood of bulls and goats could not take away sins"
3. Hebrews 10:1 (ESV) "Shadow of good things to come"
4. Isaiah 53:4
5. John 19:4 "I find no fault in him"
6. John 19:2 "crown of thorns"
7. John 19:15 "Take him away
8. John 19:30 "It is finished"

9.   Hebrews 8:1, 9:11, 24 "Great High Priest/Final Atonement"

10. Hebrews 9:17 "New covenant only goes in force when the testator dies"

11. Hebrews 12:2 "Author and finisher of our faith"

12. 2 Corinthians 5:19

Chapter 9: The Logging Camp & the Cant Hook

1.   Genesis 45:27 "The spirit of Jacob revived"

2.   John 11:21 (NIV)

3.   Genesis 3:12 (ESV)

4.   Genesis 22:1-14

5.   Psalm 56:8 (NLT) "Tears in your bottle"

6.   John 19:30 "It is finished"

7.   Philippians 3:14

8.   Romans 8:18

Chapter 10: The Key Log

1.   Genesis 3:6 "Original sin" or "Ancestral sin"

2.   Romans 5:12 "All have sinned"

3.   Genesis 3:15 "Promise of the Redeemer"

4.   Revelation 13:8 "Lamb slain from the foundation of the world"

5.   I Samuel 17 "David & Goliath"

6.   John 3:14 "Moses lifted up the serpent"

7.   John 1:1 "The Word was God"

8.   John 1:29 "Lamb of God"

9.   I Peter 4:6, Ephesians 4:9, Revelation 1:18 "Jesus went to hell to take back the keys"

10. Luke 23:43 "This day thou shalt be with me in paradise"

11. Psalm 139:8

12. John 12:24

13. John 3:6-7

14. Romans 5:18

15. Acts 1:8

16. Romans 7:24

17. Genesis 3:8-10

18. Genesis 3:23

19. John 8:1-11 "Woman caught in adultery"

20. Jeremiah 17:10, 13

8. John 8:12 "I am the light of the world"

9. John 10:9 "I am the door"

10. John 10:11 "I am the good shepherd"

11. John 11:25 "I am the resurrection, and the life"

12. John 14:6 "I am the way, the truth, and the life"

13. John 15:5 "I am the vine"

14. John 8:58 "Before Abraham was, I am"

15. Genesis 18 "God took on the form of an Angel"

16. John 2:19

17. John 2:21

18. John 19:2 "Pressed a crown of thorns into his head"

19. John 19:2 "Put on him a purple robe"

20. John 19:3 "They smote him with their hands"

21. John 19:6 "His own people rejected him"

22. Isaiah 53:4 "Smitten of God and afflicted"

23. John 19:17 "Carried his own cross"

24. Matthew 27:35-37 "Soldiers gambled for his clothes"

25. John 19:29 "Gave him vinegar to drink"

26. John 19:34 "Pierced his side with a sword"

27. Matthew 26:67 "He was spat upon"

28. Matthew 17:1-3

29. Romans 8:18

30. Ephesians 1:9-10

31. Romans 8:28

32. Jeremiah 5:14 "make this people as wood"

33. Acts 14:19-2

CITED WORKS

INTRODUCTION

1. Chief Robert TallTree, "The Soul Would Have No Rainbow If...," *HowToLiveOnPurpose.com*, The TallTrees, April 24, 2013, Feb 2020

2. "The Good Grief," (Episode 24), *The RobCast,* PodBean, June 22, 2015, PodCast

3. *"Brené Brown: Rising Strong," Oprah's SuperSoul Conversations Podcast, 2019*

4. Podcast, Quote attributed to Josh Green, (source unknown)

5. Colleen Haggerty, "Forgiving the Unforgivable," Tedx Talks, Bellingham, WA, Nov 23, 2013, Speech.

6. "Time Does Not Heal All Wounds," *Dr. Phil*, CBS, WDBJ, Lynchburg, Dec 13, 2012. Television.

CHAPTER 1: GOATS, DOGS & RIVER DRIVERS

7. Michael Hoy, *Kennebec River Log Drive, Skowhegan Community History*, Maine Memory Network, n.d., web. 17 Mar. 2021; Kifner, John. "Last Log Drive in U.S. Floating to End in Maine." *The New York Times* 8 Sept. 1976, Page 37; *River Driving on the Penobscot*, The Maine Boomhouses: River Driving History, n.d, web. 20 Feb. 2020.

8. "River Log Drive," Forest History Society, Feb 3, 2009. YouTube. Documentary Film; "Clearwater River Log Drives, Forest History Society, Dec 7, 2017. YouTube. Documentary Film, Idaho; "The Last Log Drive," video edited for Maine's PBS affiliate, MPBN. Dec 20, 2008. Documentary Style Video. Maine. YouTube.

9. "River Log Drive," Forest History Society, Feb 3, 2009. YouTube. Documentary Film; "Clearwater River Log Drives, Forest History Society, Dec 7, 2017. YouTube. Documentary Film, Idaho; "The Last Log Drive," Kris Bridges, video edited for Maine's PBS affiliate, MPBN. Dec 20, 2008. Documentary Style Video. Maine. YouTube.

10. "The Last Log Drive," Kris Bridges, video edited for Maine's PBS affiliate, MPBN. Dec 20, 2008. Documentary Style Video. Maine. YouTube; Kifner, John. "Last Log Drive in U.S. Floating to End in Maine." *The New York Times* 8 Sept. 1976, Page 37. Web.

11. "The Last Log Drive," Kris Bridges, video edited for Maine's PBS affiliate, MPBN. Dec 20, 2008. Documentary Style Video. Maine. YouTube; Kifner

12. Strong, James. "Skandalon." (#4625). Strong's Exhaustive Concordance of the Bible. Abingdon Press, 1890. Web.

13. Orr, James, M.A., D.D. General Editor. "Entry for 'MEPHIBOSHETH'." "International Standard Bible Encyclopedia." 1915; Bible Gateway, Encyclopedia of the Bible – *Merib-Baal.* Web.

CHAPTER 2: PICKAROON POLES & PEAVEY HOOKS

14. Serraf, Menachem, "What Is Tzitzit (and Tallit)?" 1993-2022 Chabad-Lubavitch Media Center. www.chabad.org. Jewish Library. (Site: Chabad.org is a division of the Chabad-Lubavitch Media Center – Under the auspices of the Lubavitch World Headquarters in everlasting memory of our founder, Rabbi Yosef Y. Kazen, pioneer of Torah, Judaism and Jewish information on the web.)

15. "Tzitziyot Workshop," Beth Shalom Messianic Congregation, (MTOI.org). Nov 11, 2016. YouTube; "Tekhelet: The Mystery of the Long-Lost Biblical Blue Thread," 1993-2022 Chabad-Lubavitch Media Center. www.chabad.org. Jewish Library. (Site: Chabad.org is a division of the Chabad-Lubavitch Media Center – Under the auspices of the Lubavitch World Headquarters in everlasting memory of our founder, Rabbi Yosef Y. Kazen, pioneer of Torah, Judaism and Jewish information on the web.)

16. *Shamash*, (jel.jewish-languages.org); "Tzitziyot Workshop," Beth Shalom Messianic Congregation, (MTOI.org). Nov 11, 2016. YouTube.

17. Strong, James. "Orphanos." Strong's Exhaustive Concordance of the Bible. Greek NT. (#3737), Abingdon Press, 1890. Web. Comforter.

18. Holy Bible, New International Version, NIV Copyright 1973, 1978, 1984, 2011 by Biblica, Inc. (Romans 12:2 NIV).

19. Holy Bible, New King James Version. Copyright 1982 by Thomas Nelson. (Numbers 11:5 NKJV).

20. Brené Brown. *"Daring Greatly: How the Courage to Be Vulnerable Transforms the Way We Live, Love, Parent, and Lead,"* AVERY an imprint of Penguin Random House New York, Paperback, April 2015.; "Atlas of the Heart," Brene Brown, HBO Max (TV Series 2022).

21. Leaf, Caroline. *Switch On Your Brain: The Key to Peak Happiness, Thinking, and Health / Dr. Caroline Leaf.* Published by Baker Books, a division of Baker Publishing Group, Paperback Edition Published 2015. (P. 35)

22. Leaf, Caroline. *Switch On Your Brain: The Key to Peak Happiness, Thinking, and Health / Dr. Caroline Leaf.* Published by Baker Books, a division of Baker Publishing Group, Paperback Edition Published 2015. (P. 33)

23. The Berean Bible, Berean Study Bible, Copyright 2016, 2020 by Bible Hub and Berean.Bible. (I Thes. 5:19 BSB).

24. "Meaning of Communications Utilizing Your Emotions," Tony Robbins, Tony Robbins For Success, Apr 16, 2015. YouTube. Speech.

25. Rabbi Pesach Wolicki, El Shaddai Ministries - Christian/Jewish Relations, Mar 22, 2018. YouTube. (Interview with Pastor Mark Biltz).

26. Osteen, Joel. *Becoming a Better You: 7 Keys to Improving Your Life Every Day.* Free Press, a Division of Simon & Schuster, Inc. Copyright 2007 by Joel Osteen. FIRST FREE PRESS trade paperback edition Aug 2009. (P.60).

27. Thomson, Helen. *"Study of Holocaust Survivors Finds Trauma Passed on to Children's Genes,"* The Guardian, Issued Fri 21 Aug 2015 13.40 EDT. (Web).

28. Thomson, Helen. *"Study of Holocaust Survivors Finds Trauma Passed on to Children's Genes,"* The Guardian, Issued Fri 21 Aug 2015 13.40 EDT. (Web).

29. Kifner, John. "Last Log Drive in U.S. Floating to End in Maine." *The New York Times* 8 Sept. 1976, Page 37. Web; ARC Identifier 13585 / Local Identifier 95.287 - Department of Agriculture. Forest Service. Division of State and Private Forestry. Fire and Aviation Management Staff. (1986) – *From Stump to Ship: A 1930 logging film,* PublicResourceOrg, Apr 15, 2010. YouTube. (Peavey Hook – Tool of a River Driver).

30. Kifner, John. "Last Log Drive in U.S. Floating to End in Maine." *The New York Times* 8 Sept. 1976, Page 37. Web; ARC Identifier 13585 / Local Identifier 95.287 - Department of Agriculture. Forest Service.

Division of State and Private Forestry. Fire and Aviation Management Staff. (1986) – *From Stump to Ship: A 1930 logging film*, PublicResourceOrg, Apr 15, 2010. YouTube. (Pickaroon Pole – Tool of a River Driver).

CHAPTER 3: SPLASH DAMS & THREE JAMS

31. ARC Identifier 13585 / Local Identifier 95.287 - Department of Agriculture. Forest Service. Division of State and Private Forestry. Fire and Aviation Management Staff. (1986) – *From Stump to Ship: A 1930 logging film*, PublicResourceOrg, Apr 15, 2010. YouTube. (Types of Log Jams).

32. Holy Bible, New International Version, NIV Copyright 1973, 1978, 1984, 2011 by Biblica, Inc. (Is. 43:18 NIV).

33. Shared by Jay Shetty during Jamie Kern Lima's Inspirational book release on the set of Tony Robbins, *"Believe It: How to Go from Underestimated to Unstoppable."* March 2021, Original Source the Buddha.

34. Holy Bible, New International Version, NIV Copyright 1973, 1978, 1984, 2011 by Biblica, Inc. (Is. 61:7 NIV).

35. Westgate, Francine. *"In the Land of Canaan: A Little Girl's Giants."* Memoir, excerpt, unpublished, (plans to publish).

CHAPTER 4: JONAH & THE LOG JAM

36. Orr, James, M.A., D.D. General Editor. "Entry for 'SHEOL'." "International Standard Bible Encyclopedia." 1915.

37. Strong, James. "Nefesh." (#5315). Strong's Exhaustive Concordance of the Bible. Abingdon Press, 1890. Web.

38. Strong, James. "Cumi/cum" (2891), "Quwm/qum (6966)," "Koum/kumi." Strong's Exhaustive Concordance of the Bible. Abingdon Press, 1890. Web; "The Resurrection of Jesus and the Sign of Jonah," Catholic Productions by Brant Pitre, Catholicproductions.com, Nov 12, 2018. YouTube. Blog.

39. Bell, Rob. *What Is the Bible?: How an Ancient Library of Poems, Letters, and Stories Can Transform the Way You Think and Feel About Everything.* Harper One, An Imprint of Harper Collins Publishers. First Edition. Copyright 2019 by WORB, Inc. (P. 102).

40. Mark, Joshua J. "Ashurnasirpal II." *World History Encyclopedia*. World History Encyclopedia, 09 Jul 2014. Web. 15 Apr 2022.

CHAPTER 5: ASH POLES & LOG BOOMS

41. Westgate, Francine. *"In the Land of Canaan: A Little Girl's Giants."* Memoir, excerpt, unpublished, (plans to publish).

CHAPTER 6: A LION IN CORK BOOTS

42. "Loggers' Boots." *Logger's Boots or Cork Boots - Nail Soled Boots for Lumberjacks*, Mendocino Coast Model Railroad & Historical Society, n.d., https://www.mendorailhistory.org/1_logging/log_boots.htm.; Mary Garrison, "The River Pigs of Logging," *Spokane Historical*, n.d., accessed April 16, 2022, https://spokanehistorical.org/items/show/587.

43. Vine's Expository Dictionary of New Testament Words. A-13,Verb,G4862, *sunallasso*.

44. Jeremiah K. Garrett, "The 5 Offerings in the Old Testament." Seedbed, July 29, 2014, accessed April 16, 2022, https://seedbed.com/5-offerings-old-testament/

45. Bibliatodo, Permission to Distribute given to Joseph Olvera. The Orthodox Jewish Bible, Copyright 2002, 2003, AFI International Publishers, https://www.bibliatodo.com/en/the-bible/orthodox-jewish-bible/genesis-4 (Gen. 4:7 OJB).

46. Eli Lizorkin-Eyzenberg, Dean of the Jewish Studies faculty at eTeacher, http://lp.eteacherbiblical.com/lp_biblical_hebrew_sin-en.html?blog=1; Jovial Cynic, "Cain's Sacrifice," Newprotest.org: a healthy criticism of everything, October 03, 2015, accessed April 14, 2022.; Brown, Driver, Briggs and Genesis. "Hebrew Lexicon entry for Chatta'ah." "The KJV Old Testament Hebrew Lexicon."

47. "Guideposts." *Guideposts Classics: Corrie ten Boom on Forgiveness*, https://www.guideposts.org/better-living/positive-living/guideposts-classics-corrie-ten-boom-forgiveness; Guideposts Classics: Corrie ten Boom on Forgiveness & Bible.org/Corrie ten Boom, Feb 2, 2009; Corrie ten Boom with John and Elizabeth Sherrill, *"The Hiding Place,"* Spire Books, Fleming H. Revell Company, copyright 1971, printed in U.S.A.

48. "Guideposts." *Guideposts Classics: Corrie ten Boom on Forgiveness*, https://www.guideposts.org/better-living/positive-living/guideposts-

classics-corrie-ten-boom-forgiveness; Guideposts Classics: Corrie ten Boom on Forgiveness & Bible.org/Corrie ten Boom, Feb 2, 2009; Corrie ten Boom with John and Elizabeth Sherrill, *The Hiding Place,* Spire Books, Fleming H. Revell Company, copyright 1971, printed in U.S.A.

CHAPTER 7: DONKEY ENGINES & WANNIGANS

49. David Wilma, HistoryLink.org Essay 5331, "John Dobeer invents the donkey engine and revolutionizes logging in August 1881." Posted 03/01/2003. Last updated July 2, 2008, https://www.historylink.org/File/5331; "Steam Donkeys." *Steam Donkey Engines*, Mendocino Coast Model Railroad & Historical Society, n.d., https://www.mendorailhistory.org/1_logging/steam_donkeys.htm

50. "Skid Roads." *Skid Roads*, Mendocino Coast Model Railroad & Historical Society, n.d., https://www.mendorailhistory.org/1_railroads/skid_oxen_roads.htm; American Heritage® Dictionary of the English Language, Fifth Edition. Copyright ©2016 by Houghton Mifflin Harcourt Publishing Company. Published by Houghton Mifflin Harcourt Publishing Company.

51. "Jewish Festival." In Judaism: The Jewish Holidays, by Editors of Encyclopaedia Britannica, https://www.britannica.com/topic/Jewish-festivals; Mark Biltz, "The Feasts of the Lord – Part 1of 4 – Spring: Passover to Pentecost, Mar 11, 2018, Allison Shatter, YouTube; Mark Biltz, *"Feast of the Lord – Yom Teruah Feast of Trumpets – Part 2 of 4,* March 11, 2018, Allison Shatter, YouTube; Mark Biltz, "Feasts of the Lord - Day Atonement Yom Kippur - Part 3 of 4, Mar 11, 2018, Allison Shatter, YouTube; Mark Biltz, *"Feasts of the Lord – Sukkot Feast of Tabernacles – Part 4 of 4,"* Apr 11, 2018, Allison Shatter, YouTube.

52. Blue Letter Bible, *"Mikrah,"* (Strong, James. H4744 – Strong's Hebrew Lexicon Number), https://studybible.info/strongs/H4744; Mark Biltz, "The Feasts of the Lord – Part 1of 4 – Spring: Passover to Pentecost, Mar 11, 2018, Allison Shatter, YouTube; Mark Biltz, *"Feast of the Lord – Yom Teruah Feast of Trumpets – Part 2 of 4,* March 11, 2018, Allison Shatter YouTube Channel; Mark Biltz, "Feasts of the Lord - Day Atonement Yom Kippur - Part 3 of 4, Mar 11, 2018, Allison

Shatter, YouTube; Mark Biltz, *"Feasts of the Lord – Sukkot Feast of Tabernacles – Part 4 of 4,"* Apr 11, 2018, Allison Shatter, YouTube; Rob Bell, *"The Goat Has Left The Building,"* Apr 5, 2014, John Zylka, YouTube.

53. Shmuel Kogan, *"Passover: When did we begin observing Passover? Did we celebrate it during the forty years of wandering in the desert?"* Chabad.org, n.d., https://www.chabad.org/holidays/passover/pesach_cdo/aid/522662/jewish/When-did-we-begin-observing-Passover.htm; The Temple Institute, "Historic Practice Passover Offering," A Film of the Practice of Passover Offering, The Temple Institute Conducts Unprecedented Passover Offering Practice Drill, Mar 30, 2015, Youtube. (I thirst, give the lamb a drink), https://www.youtube.com/watch?v=5kgbRusmqjs

54. Mordecai Griffin, "Yom Kippur: The 7 Secrets," Lapid Judaism, Oct 5, 2019, https://www.youtube.com/watch?v=Ilpm6sCUv-A, YouTube.

55. N.T. Wright. N.T. Wright Online & The Wisconsin Center for Christian Studies, *"Tracing Atonement Through the Story of Scripture,"* Copyright 2018, https://www.ntwrightonline.org/tracing-atonement-through-the-story-of-scripture/

56. N.T. Wright. N.T. Wright Online & The Wisconsin Center for Christian Studies, *"Tracing Atonement Through the Story of Scripture,"* Copyright 2018, https://www.ntwrightonline.org/tracing-atonement-through-the-story-of-scripture/

57. N.T. Wright. N.T. Wright Online & The Wisconsin Center for Christian Studies, *"Tracing Atonement Through the Story of Scripture,"* Copyright 2018, https://www.ntwrightonline.org/tracing-atonement-through-the-story-of-scripture/

58. Sarah E. Fisher and hebrewwordlessons.com, *"Bethlehem: Oh Little House of Bread,"* Hebrew Word Lessons: Understanding the Hebrew Bible one Word at a time, Dec 17, 2017, https://hebrewwordlessons.com/2017/12/17/bethlehem-oh-little-house-of-bread/, (*Bet Lekhem or Bet Lachem*).

59. Ray Vander Laan. *"The Bible from Jesus' Culture Perspective 2000 Years Ago,"* Jul 1, 2013, https://www.youtube.com/watch?v=tE5xyKdIeXM, YouTube.

60. Daily Renewal for Pastors. *"490-The Number of Perfection,"* Church Source: HarperCollins Christian Publishing, n.d., https://media.harpercollinschristian.com/email/pastors-devo/18-Feb; Kathie Lee Gifford with Jason Sobel, *"The Rock, the Road, and the Rabb: My Journey into the Heart of Scriptural Faith and the Land Where It All Began,"* Nelson, Thomas, Inc. Edition Reprint, 03/05/2019; Jason Sobel, *"70X7=Forgiveness,"* Rabbi Jason Sobel, Sep 22, 2016. Youtube.

61. NASB 1995: New American Standard Bible – NASB 1995, New American Standard Bible Copyright © 1960, 1962, 1963, 1968, 1971, 1972, 1973, 1975, 1977, 1995, 2020 by The Lockman Foundation (Matt. 18:21 NASB)

62. Holy Bible, New International Version, NIV Copyright 1973, 1978, 1984, 2011 by Biblica, Inc. (Matt. 18:23-35 NIV).

63. R.T. Kendall. "Total Forgiveness," Charisma House, A Strang Company, Copyright 2002, 2007, (P.9).

64. Mordecai Griffin, "Yom Kippur: The 7 Secrets," Lapid Judaism, Oct 5, 2019, https://www.youtube.com/watch?v=Ilpm6sCUv-A, YouTube.

65. "Brené Brown: Rising Strong," *Oprah's SuperSoul Conversations Podcast*, 2019 (A conspiracy theory).

66. "Brené Brown: Rising Strong," *Oprah's SuperSoul Conversations Podcast*, 2019 (A confabulation).

67. Holy Bible, New International Version, NIV Copyright 1973, 1978, 1984, 2011 by Biblica, Inc. (Matt. 5:23-26 NIV).

68. Holy Bible, New International Version, NIV Copyright 1973, 1978, 1984, 2011 by Biblica, Inc. (Lk. 6:32-36 NIV).

69. The Berean Bible, Berean Study Bible, Copyright 2016, 2020 by Bible Hub and Berean.Bible. (Col. 3:13 BSB).

70. The Holy Bible, English Standard Version. ESV® Text Edition: 2016. Copyright © 2001 by Crossway Bibles, a publishing ministry of Good News Publishers. (Eph. 4:32 ESV).

71. Holy Bible, New International Version, NIV Copyright 1973, 1978, 1984, 2011 by Biblica, Inc. (Matt. 5:23-24 NIV).

72. Gabrielle Meyer, Logging, Mississippi River, Wannigan, Sept 14, 2017, https://www.hhhistory.com/2017/09/river-wannigan.html; ARC

Identifier 13585 / Local Identifier 95.287 - Department of Agriculture. Forest Service. Division of State and Private Forestry. Fire and Aviation Management Staff. (1986) – *From Stump to Ship: A 1930 logging film*, PublicResourceOrg, Apr 15, 2010. YouTube. (Four meals a day).

CHAPTER 8: THE SCAPEGOAT & THE RIVER DRIVER

73. Rob Bell, *"The Goat Has Left The Building,"* Apr 5, 2014, John Zylka, YouTube. (*Azazel*, Scapegoat); "Scapegoat," Definition of Scapegoat, History of Scapegoat, Merriam-Webster, Since 1828, https://www.merriam-webster.com/dictionary/scapegoat.

74. Blue Letter Bible. Lexicon: Strong, James, Strong's H5375 – *Nasa*, https://www.blueletterbible.org/lexicon/h5375/kjv/wlc/0-1/ (to lift, bear up, carry, take).

75. The Holy Bible, English Standard Version. ESV® Text Edition: 2016. Copyright © 2001 by Crossway Bibles, a publishing ministry of Good News Publishers. (Heb 10:1 ESV).

76. Jack Moline. Prayerbook Vocabulary Studies, P101-Tammu, June 18, 2009, Rabbi Jack Moline, https://leaches.net/moline/torah--162.html; Rob Bell, *"The Goat Has Left The Building,"* Apr 5, 2014, John Zylka, YouTube; Michael Maynard, "It Is Finished…The Last Words of Jesus," June 25m 2017, https://www.sweetwaternow.com/it-is-finished-the-last-words-of-jesus/#:~:text=Tetelestai – The Sacrifice Is Accomplished, the Old Testament sacrificial system.

CHAPTER 9: THE LOGGING CAMP & THE CANT HOOK

77. "Brené Brown: Rising Strong," *Oprah's SuperSoul Conversations* Podcast, 2019

78. "The Good Grief," (Episode 24), *The RobCast*, PodBean, June 22, 2015, PodCast

79. Maine Forestry, *"A Loggers Life in the Maine Woods,"* https://www.maineforestry.net/single-post/2015/09/06/a-loggers-life-in-the-maine-woods, n.d.

80. Pesach Wolicki. "Cup of Salvation: A Powerful Journey Through King David's Psalms of Praise," CJCUC Publishing House, The Center for Jewish-Christian Understanding & Cooperation (CJCUC), Copyright 2017. (P. 84, 85, 86); Jen Wilkin, "God of Creation: A Study of Genesis 1-11," Published by LifeWay Press, 2017 Jen Wilkin, Reprinted July

2018, week 3 video; Rob Bell, "What is Bible?", Harper Collins
Publishers, Copyright 2017 by WORB, Inc. (P. 107, 108

81. Pesach Wolicki. "Cup of Salvation: A Powerful Journey Through King
David's Psalms of Praise," CJCUC Publishing House, The Center for
Jewish-Christian Understanding & Cooperation (CJCUC), Copyright
2017. (To a pagan mindset…P. 86)

82. Unknown Source. Quote, "Your tears water the ground around your feet
so that something new can grow."

83. Sarah Montana, "Why Forgiveness is Worth It," TedxLincolnSquare,
an independent event, NY, Mar 2018, Speech.

84. Sarah Montana, "Why Forgiveness is Worth It," TedxLincolnSquare,
an independent event, NY, Mar 2018, Speech. (Quote: How do you
forgive effectively…).

85. *Story removed during final edits

86. Elin Nordegren, Excerpts from Elin Nordegren interview with People
magazine, by Associated Press, August 25, 2010, "Forgiveness takes
time…" https://www.golfchannel.com/article/associated-press/excerpts-
elin-nordegren-interview-
people#:~:text=%E2%80%9CForgiveness%20takes%20time.,be%20ha
ppy%20in%20the%20future.

87. Jonah Nelson. *What Hand Tool is Used to Roll Logs?* Cant Hooks
and Peaveys: Similarities and Differences, TheArtOfHandTools.com,
https://theartofhandtools.com/what-hand-tool-is-used-to-roll-logs/, n.d.

CHAPTER 10: THE KEY LOG

88. ARC Identifier 13585 / Local Identifier 95.287 - Department of
Agriculture. Forest Service. Division of State and Private Forestry. Fire
and Aviation Management Staff. (1986) – *From Stump to Ship: A 1930
logging film*, PublicResourceOrg, Apr 15, 2010. YouTube; "River Log
Drive," Forest History Society, Feb 3, 2009. YouTube. Documentary
Film; Mary Grow. *"Up and down the Kennebec Valley: Log drives and
harvesting "frozen gold,"* The Town Line Since 1989, April 14, 2022,
https://townline.org/up-and-down-the-kennebec-valley-log-drives-and-
harvesting-frozen-gold/, (Key Log).

89. Ray Vander Laan. *"The Bible from Jesus' Culture Perspective 2000 Years Ago,"* Jul 1, 2013, https://www.youtube.com/watch?v=tE5xyKdIeXM, YouTube.

90. ABC News, "Sheep's blood provides rattlesnake anti-venom, May 22, 2005, https://www.abc.net.au.

91. Mordecai Griffin, "Yom Kippur: The 7 Secrets," Lapid Judaism, Oct 5, 2019, https://www.youtube.com/watch?v=Ilpm6sCUv-A, YouTube.

92. Brené Brown. *"Daring Greatly: How the Courage to Be Vulnerable Transforms the Way We Live, Love, Parent, and Lead,"* AVERY an imprint of Penguin Random House New York, Paperback, April 2015. (Shame has two tapes…).

93. Sheila Walsh, Former Host of 700 Club, Talks About Her Battle with Depression, Jun 22, 2015, https://www.youtube.com/watch?v=g2FWqKuglFs

94. Brené Brown. *"Daring Greatly: How the Courage to Be Vulnerable Transforms the Way We Live, Love, Parent, and Lead,"* AVERY an imprint of Penguin Random House New York, Paperback, April 2015. (The intensely painful feeling or experience…).

95. Brené Brown. *"Daring Greatly: How the Courage to Be Vulnerable Transforms the Way We Live, Love, Parent, and Lead,"* AVERY an imprint of Penguin Random House New York, Paperback, April 2015. (Shame started as a two person…).

96. Edward T. Welch, *"Shame Interrupted: How God Lifts the Pain of Worthlessness and Rejection,"* New Growth Press, April 30, 2012. (Quote: Shame is life-dominating and stubborn…).

97. Michael Meadows, Quote: "Unforgiveness is when you freezeframe someone in their weakness."

98. W. Doyle Gentry. *"When Someone You Love Is Angry: A 7-Step Program for Dealing with Toxic Anger and Taking Back Control of Your Life,"* The Berkley Publishing Group, Published by the Penguin Group, Penguin Group, Inc., Print, Paperback, Sept 2004. (All a grown up is…).

99. *Holy Bible: New Living Translation.* 2015. Carol Stream, IL: Tyndale House Publishers. As found in the Logos Bible study software program. (NLT: I Cor 11:27).

100. Brené Brown. *"The Gifts of Imperfection: Let Go of Who You Think You're Supposed to Be and Embrace Who You Are,"* Hazelden Publishing, Print, Paperback, 2010. (Quote: Wholehearted living is about engaging in our lives…).

101. Brené Brown. *"Daring Greatly: How the Courage to Be Vulnerable Transforms the Way We Live, Love, Parent, and Lead,"* AVERY an imprint of Penguin Random House New York, Paperback, April 2015. (P.11).

102. Ruth Graham Lotz, Liberty University Convocation, Dec 2, 2009, Speech.

103. Brené Brown. *"Daring Greatly: How the Courage to Be Vulnerable Transforms the Way We Live, Love, Parent, and Lead,"* AVERY an imprint of Penguin Random House New York, Paperback, April 2015.

104. Judaism Ritual Life, "Circling Wedding Ritual Makes a Comeback," Philadelphia Jewish Exponent, Mid-Atlantic Media, by Joeyjojojr01, Mar 20, 2014, https://www.jewishexponent.com/2014/03/20/circling-wedding-ritual-makes-a-comeback/

105. Mark Biltz. *"The Feasts of the Lord – Part 2 – Feast of Trumpets – Rosh Hashanah,"* May 24, 2021, MFA Pictures, https://www.youtube.com/watch?v=YcQEzq3Z-24

106. Brené Brown. *"Daring Greatly: How the Courage to Be Vulnerable Transforms the Way We Live, Love, Parent, and Lead,"* AVERY an imprint of Penguin Random House New York, Paperback, April 2015, (Vulnerability. *Vulnerare*).

107. Tracey R. Rich. *"Days of Awe,"* 10 Days of Awe, Judaism 101, https://www.jewfaq.org/days-of-awe, date accessed April 17, 2017.

108. Mordecai Griffin, "Yom Kippur: The 7 Secrets," Lapid Judaism, Oct 5, 2019, https://www.youtube.com/watch?v=Ilpm6sCUv-A, YouTube, (Day of Atonement and Grafting).

109. "Decision," *Decidere,* https://www.vocabulary.com/dictionary/decision#:~:text=Decision%20originally%20comes%20from%20the%20Latin%20decidere%20(%22determine%22). (To cut).

110. Mike Norton. "Fighting For Redemption, AuthorHouse, Print, Hardcover, Jan 10, 2011, Quote, (Few suffer more…).

111. "Robert Green Ingersoll Quotes." BrainyQuote.com. BrainyMedia Inc, 2022. 17 April 2022. https://www.brainyquote.com/quotes/robert_green_ingersoll_149234

112. "William Westgate Quote." Associate Pastor, The Ramp Church International, "Sorry shifts the atmosphere."

113. *Quote removed during final edits

CHAPTER 11: THE MILL

114. Westgate, Francine. *"In the Land of Canaan: A Little Girl's Giants."* Memoir, excerpt, unpublished, (plans to publish).

115. "Mark Twain Quotes." BrainyQuote.com. BrainyMedia Inc, 2022. 17 April 2022. https://www.brainyquote.com/quotes/mark_twain_109919

116. Bailey, Regina. "The Olfactory System and Your Sense of Smell." ThoughtCo, Aug. 17, 2021, thoughtco.com/olfactory-system-4066176.

117. Mordecai Griffin, "Yom Kippur: The 7 Secrets," Lapid Judaism, Oct 5, 2019, https://www.youtube.com/watch?v=Ilpm6sCUv-A, YouTube, (Day of Atonement and Grafting).

118. Mordecai Griffin, "Yom Kippur: The 7 Secrets," Lapid Judaism, Oct 5, 2019, https://www.youtube.com/watch?v=Ilpm6sCUv-A, YouTube, (Day of Atonement and Grafting).

119. Mordecai Griffin, "Yom Kippur: The 7 Secrets," Lapid Judaism, Oct 5, 2019, https://www.youtube.com/watch?v=Ilpm6sCUv-A, YouTube, (Day of Atonement and Grafting).

CHAPTER 12: CLEANING THE REAR

120. "The Last Log Drive," Kris Bridges, video edited for Maine's PBS affiliate, MPBN. Dec 20, 2008. Documentary Style Video. Maine. YouTube; Kifner, John. "Last Log Drive in U.S. Floating to End in Maine." *The New York Times* 8 Sept. 1976, Page 37, https://www.nytimes.com/1976/09/08/archives/last-log-drive-in-us-floating-to-end-in-maine.html

121. Westgate, Francine. *"In the Land of Canaan: A Little Girl's Giants."* Memoir, excerpt, unpublished, (plans to publish).

CHAPTER 13: BOATS, ROPES & HOPE

122. "The Last Log Drive," Kris Bridges, video edited for Maine's PBS affiliate, MPBN. Dec 20, 2008. Documentary Style Video. Maine. YouTube; ARC Identifier 13585 / Local Identifier 95.287 - Department

of Agriculture. Forest Service. Division of State and Private Forestry. Fire and Aviation Management Staff. (1986) – *From Stump to Ship: A 1930 logging film*, PublicResourceOrg, Apr 15, 2010. YouTube. (Line attached to the wooden boats, anchored to shore).

123. Orr, James, M.A., D.D. General Editor. "Entry for 'TIKVAH; TIKVATH'." "International Standard Bible Encyclopedia." 1915; Abarim Publications – Tikvah meaning, Etymology of the name Tikvah, last updated on Feb 14, 2022, https://www.abarim-publications.com/Meaning/Tikvah.html; Brown-Driver-Briggs Hebrew and English Lexicon, Unabridged, Electronic Database, Copyright 2022, 2033, 2006 by Biblesoft, Inc, Strong's Exhaustive Concordance #8615. tiqvah, https://biblehub.com/hebrew/8615.htm

124. Lewis B. Smedes, *"Forgive and Forget: Healing the Hurts We Don't Deserve,"* HarperCollins Publishers, publication date: Sept 25, 2007.

125. Holy Bible, New International Version, NIV Copyright 1973, 1978, 1984, 2011 by Biblica, Inc. (Matt 1:1-5 NIV).

126. "Oxgoad." Merriam-Webster.com Dictionary, Merriam-Webster, https://www.merriam-webster.com/dictionary/oxgoad. Accessed 17 Apr. 2022.

127. Lillian Disney Interview - Oct 1982, by Jim Korkis, contributing writer, May 6, 2015, MousePlanet, https://www.mouseplanet.com/11006/Lillian_Disney_Interview__October_1982

128. James E. Faust, "The Healing Power of Forgiveness," The Church of Jesus Christ of Latter-Day Saints, Quotes Dr. Sidney Simon, https://www.churchofjesuschrist.org/study/general-conference/2007/04/the-healing-power-of-forgiveness?lang=eng, (Forgiveness is freeing up and putting…)

CHAPTER 14: ROUGH WATERS, SMOOTH LOGS, ALL THINGS

129. David, by Michelangelo, Michelangelo Paintings, Sculptures, Biography, https://www.michelangelo.org/david.jsp, n.d., Accessed Oct 2021.

130. Bell, Rob. *"Drops Like Stars: A Few Thoughts on Creativity and Suffering"* Zondervan, Paperback, Oct 9, 2010. (Quote: His David was in the stone…P.76).

131. *River Driving on the Penobscot*, The Maine Boomhouses: River Driving History, n.d, web. 20 Feb. 2020. (Logging companies, markings, ownership).

132. "Theophany." Merriam-Webster.com Dictionary, Merriam-Webster, https://www.merriam-webster.com/dictionary/theophany. Accessed 18 Apr. 2022.

133. Frankl, E. Viktor. "Man's Search for Meaning," Verlag fur Jugend und Volk (Austria), Beacon Press (English), Publication date 1946 (Vienna, Austria), 1959 (United States), Second edition (1947). (Suffering ceases to be suffering...).

134. Bell, Rob. *What Is the Bible?: How an Ancient Library of Poems, Letters, and Stories Can Transform the Way You Think and Feel About Everything.* Harper One, An Imprint of Harper Collins Publishers. First Edition. Copyright 2019 by WORB, Inc.

135. Bell, Rob. *What Is the Bible?: How an Ancient Library of Poems, Letters, and Stories Can Transform the Way You Think and Feel About Everything.* Harper One, An Imprint of Harper Collins Publishers. First Edition. Copyright 2019 by WORB, Inc.

About the Author

Francine Westgate is an inspirational speaker, teacher, and author. She holds her minister's license through One Way Churches International under the leadership of Bishop Lorenzo Hall and Bishop S.Y. Younger. She is the wife of Pastor William Westgate, Associate Pastor of the RAMP Church International. Together they have three sons and one granddaughter. Francine and her husband lead the married Couples ministry, where they teach couples how to maintain a healthy marriage by sharing their own personal experiences. Francine has a successful blog called "I Am M.O.R.E" and has two memoirs in the works, *In the Land of Canaan: A Little Girl's Giants* and *Fiddleheads*, where she shares how she overcame the crippling effects of childhood sexual abuse through hope and the power of forgiveness. Francine also shares her wisdom and knowledge as she leads the Refreshed Women's Group at the RAMP Church International in Lynchburg, VA. Francine continues to travel and teaches workshops on forgiveness, where she shares her story to empower the hurting and to help them view their wounds as a means to help others. Francine loves to study and teach the Word of God and is the director of the Christian Education Department for One Way Churches International.

Ways to contact the author:

Visit her website at www.francinewestgate.com.

Made in the USA
Middletown, DE
28 November 2022

16287430R00166